Inequality
and
Poverty
in Ethiopia

Challenges and Opportunities

Dr. Assefa Muluneh

ARCHWAY
PUBLISHING

Archway Publishing books may be ordered through booksellers or by contacting:

Archway Publishing
1663 Liberty Drive
Bloomington, IN 47403
www.archwaypublishing.com
844-669-3957

ISBN: 978-1-6657-1166-1 (sc)
ISBN: 978-1-6657-1167-8 (e)

Library of Congress Control Number: 2021918875

Print information available on the last page.

Archway Publishing rev. date: 09/21/2021

CONTENTS

LIST OF TABLES

LIST OF CHARTS

FIGURES AND APPENDICES

Abbreviations

CSA Central Statistical Agency (of Ethiopia)

CPI Corruption Perception Index

CRGE Climate Resilient Green Economy

DRs Developing Regional States

EKC Environmental Kuznets Curve

EPI Environmental Performance Index

ERHS Ethiopian Rural Household Survey

GTP Growth and Transformation Plan

HHS Household Survey

IHDP Integrated Housing Development Plan

LMIS Labor Market Information System

MDGs Millennium Development Goals

MFI Microfinance Institutions

MOFED Ministry of Finance and Economic Development

PASDEP Plan for Accelerated and Sustained Development to
End Poverty

PES Public Employment Services

SDGs Sustainable development Goals

SDPRP Sustainable Development and Poverty Reduction
Program

Currency Equivalence: 1 US$ = 44.78 Ethiopian Birr as of August
12, 2021

ACKNOWLEDGEMENTS

Mr. Seifu Yigezu has been a phenomenal role model. I acknowledge his guidance and continued support.

Professor Jeff Lloyd Dumas read the manuscript and provided invaluable suggestions, for which I am grateful.

Dr. Rosalind Williams, Dr. Costa Mazidzi, Mr. Teferra Yigezu, Mr. Steven Levine, Mr. Neal Abramson, Mr. Beruk Yemane, Mr. Geremew Mekonnen, Dr. John Grabarczyk, Dr. Arisa Ude, and Dr. Kyle Kucera have shared their wisdom and tact in communicating ideas that engage thoughtful discussions.

Mr. Girma Muluneh, Mr. Goshu Abebe, Timkhite Kullu Berhane, and the Muluneh family have provided encouragement and expressed their support.

Mrs. Bethany Berhane and Joseph, Mark, and Solomon Assefa deserve special thanks for giving me the space to focus on the book.

ACKNOWLEDGEMENTS

Mr Seth Yigezu has been a phenomenal role model. I acknowledge his guidance and continued support.

Professor Jeff Joyal Dumas read the manuscript and provided invaluable suggestions, for which I am grateful.

Dr Rosalind Williams, Dr Cosa Mandel, Ms Teluru Yigezu, Ms Steven Levine, Mr Axel Abramson, Mr Beruk Yemane, Mr Getenew Mekonnen, Dr John Grabowsky, Dr Arisa Ude, and Dr Kyle Kucera have shared their wisdom and aid in communicating ideas that engage thoughtful discussions.

Ms Girma Mulugeta, Mr Goshu Abebe, Timekhte Kifin Berhane, and the Mulunch family have provided encouragement and expressed their support.

Ms Debhury Berhane and Joseph Marki and Solomon Assen deserve special thanks for giving me the space to focus on the book.

INTRODUCTION

Inequality and poverty loom large on a global level, with less developed countries manifesting the bulk of the problem. The attempts to mitigate the problem taken by UN agencies and at the local levels have had little effect against the wave of burgeoning inequality and poverty. This reality has triggered expediency at the UN level to engage countries in a quest to eradicate poverty by 2030.

This book engages a discussion on inequality and poverty in Ethiopia and provides recommendations aimed at curbing and eventually eradicating poverty. The book is organized in seven chapters. Chapter one presents the country-background situation, the size of population and its trend, the political structure, and the economy. It sets the foundation for the ensuing chapters that are preoccupied with the assessment of the magnitude of poverty and inequality.

Chapter two focuses on income distribution, household expenditure, cost of living, health, housing, and education inequalities. Chapter three highlights the development strategies of Ethiopia between 1960 and 2020 to explore why development has failed to curb inequality and poverty. Chapter four discusses the impact of environmental degradation on the poor. Chapter five brings attention to the impact of corruption on growth and poverty.

Chapter six addresses poverty, employment, and unemployment situations at the global level and in Ethiopia. The overall assessment of the chapter will provide a better picture in terms of understanding the labor market situation and poverty trend in Ethiopia to propose practical recommendations. The final chapter includes summary and poverty reduction strategies.

CHAPTER I

Country Background Situation, Population, Political Structure, and the Economy

1. Introduction

Ethiopia is the second most populous country in Africa, and twelfth in the world, with a total population of 114.96 million. Between 2015 and 2019, it emerged as a vibrant economy with an average GDP growth rate of 8.9 percent. The country also rolled out a series of development programs to tackle poverty. However, poverty still looms large.

This chapter introduces background information about Ethiopia and its evolving political structure, followed by an assessment of the direction of the economy, income distribution, and international trade. This chapter also establishes a foundation for ensuing chapters, which focus on the assessment of poverty and inequality in Ethiopia, concluding with recommendations aimed at curbing and eradicating poverty.

2. Country Background Situation

Ethiopia is an ancient independent country, located in the Horn of Africa with a land area of 1,000,000 square kilometers (386,102 square miles). The capital city, Addis Ababa, hosts international headquarters. The Economic Commission for Africa, and the Organization of African Unity play key roles in fostering economic development and cooperation among member nations. Neighboring countries include Eritrea to the north, Somalia to the east, South Sudan to the west, and Kenya to the south.

Throughout its history, the country has hosted various racial stocks, with the earliest known inhabitants being Cushites. Later, Hamitic people from the north flourished there. Naturally, these racial stocks resulted in different ethnic formations. The major ethnic groups are the Amharas, the Oromos, the Tigres, and the Guraghes.[1] Ethiopia is also a mosaic of languages. Encyclopedia Britannica identifies about a hundred languages spoken in Ethiopia.[2] However, the website "Ethiopian Treasures" lists "86 distinct languages and as many as two hundred dialects."[3] Amharic is the official language of Ethiopia.

Orthodox Christianity is the predominant religion (43.1%), followed by Islam (34.1%), Protestantism (19.4%), traditional beliefs (1.5%), Roman Catholicism (0.9%), and other religions

---

[1] Encyclopedia Americana (vol. 10, 1966), 543.

[2] Encyclopedia Britannica. Retrieved from: https://www.britannica.com/place/Ethiopia/Ethnic-groups-and-languages.

[3] Ethiopian Treasures. Retrieved from: http://www.ethiopiantreasures.co.uk/pages/language.htm.

(1.0%).[4] The country is also recognized for its cultural and natural sites. World Heritage sites include Aksum (1980), Fasil Ghebbi, Gondar Region (1979), Harar Jugol, the Fortified Historic Town (2006), Konso Cultural Landscape (2011), Lower Valley of the Awash (1980), Lower Valley of the Omo (1980), Rock-Hewn Churches, Lalibela (1978), Tiya (1980), and The Simien National Park (1978).[5]

The lower valleys of the Awash and Omo rivers are "home to several paleoanthropological sites that have yielded remains that provide the theory of human evolution."[6] Indeed, Lucy, the oldest hominid was discovered in the Awash Valley in Ethiopia.

Major topographical features of the country are the highland complex of mountains and plateaus divided by the Rift Valley, and a series of lowlands.[7] Important rivers originate from the highlands and flow through deep gorges. The Blue Nile and its tributaries are significant rivers. Combined with Tekeze of the north and Baro of the south, they constitute around 50 percent of the outflow of water from Ethiopia. [8]

The climatic zones can be broadly grouped into three: the cold climate, the temperate climate, and the hot climate. The cold climate in the highest zone (10,000 feet) ranges from the

[4] Encyclopedia Britannica. Retrieved from: https://www.britannica.com/place/Ethiopia/Religion.

[5] UNESCO, World Heritage Center. Retrieved from: https://whc.unesco.org/en/statesparties/et.

[6] UNESCO, World Heritage Center. Retrieved from: https://whc.unesco.org/en/statesparties/et

[7] Irvin Kaplan, et al; Area Handbook of Ethiopia (Washington: US Government Printing Office, 1971), 9.

[8] Kaplan et al., 9.

freezing point to 60°F. The temperate zone (5,000–8,000 feet) has a moderate climate with a temperature of 60°F–85°F. The lowest zone (below 5,000 feet) exhibits a hot climate with a temperature of 80°F on average, although some areas register temperatures as high as 120°F. Average annual rainfall varies from 2.5 inches nearby area of the Red Sea to 106 inches in the southwest regions. The rainy season usually lasts from the middle of June to the middle of September. The other seasons exhibit dry weather.

Wild animals are predominantly found in the southern part of Ethiopia. They include elephants, lions, monkeys, and wolves. The nyala, the rarest of antelopes, is found in the remote high mountain regions.[9]

3. Population

The Ethiopian population is estimated at 114.96 million with 49.9% female and 50.1% male. Youth population aged 15–24 accounts for 21.5% of the total population; and ages 25-54 comprise 31.1%. Urban areas house 21% of the population, and rural areas house 79%. The median age is twenty, and life expectancy is sixty-six years. The average fertility rate per woman was 4.73 in the period 2016–2019, with the average rate of population growth estimated at 2.6%. Table 1 (below) captures the trend in population growth from 2010 to 2019. In 2021, Ethiopia is the twelfth most populated country in the world.

---

[9] African Wildlife Foundation. Retrieved from: https://www.awf.org/country/ethiopia

Table 1 Population Data -Ethiopia (2010–2019)

Year	Total Population	Female Population (% of total pop)	Urban Population (% of total pop)
2019	112,078,730	49.7	21.2
2018	109,224,559	49.97	20.8
2017	106,400,024	49.986	20.3
2016	103,603,501	49.996	19.9
2015	100,835,458	50.009	19.4
2014	98,094,253	50.026	19
2013	95,385,785	50.046	18.6
2012	92,726,971	50.068	18.2
2011	90,139,927	50.089	17.7
2010	87,639,964	50.106	17.3

Source: World Bank data. Retrieved from: Population, total - Ethiopia | Data (worldbank.org)
Urban population (% of total population) - Ethiopia | Data (worldbank.org)
Population, female (% of total population) - Ethiopia | Data (worldbank.org)

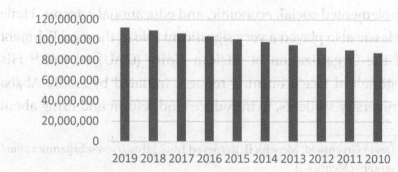

Chart created by author based on World Bank data.

4. Political Structure

Ethiopia has maintained its independence. The Ethiopians defeated Italian forces in 1896 at the Battle of Adwa under King Menelik II. "After Adwa, Menelik's Ethiopia was at once accepted by the European powers as a real political force."[10]

Ethiopia embarked on the road to modernization under the era of Menelik II, who ruled the country from 1889 to 1913. Roads and bridges were built, a postal system was organized, and telephone lines were erected. A railroad, which was started during Menelik's era, eventually linked Addis Ababa with Djibouti (a Red Sea port).[11]

Driven by a burning desire to expand its territory, Italy (again) invaded Ethiopia in 1935. However, the Ethiopian fighters waged a war of resistance and defeated the Italian forces in 1941 under Emperor Haile Selassie. Afterward, Ethiopia continued to rise on the foundation of progress it had already been building.

Emperor Haile Selassie, who ruled Ethiopia from 1930 to 1974, followed Menelik's path to modernization. He implemented social, economic, and educational reforms. Haile Selassie also played a very significant role in the establishment of the Organization of African Unity (OAU) in 1963.[12] His regime did face a burning request, initiated by Addis Ababa University students, to introduce land reform and bring about

---

[10] David Greenfield, Menelik II. Retrieved from https://www.britannica.com/biography/Menilek-II

[11] Menelik II. Retrieved from https://www.encyclopedia.com/people/history/african-history-biographies/menelik-ii

[12] "Haile Selassie: Why the African Union put up a statue," BBC News; Feb 10, 2019, https://www.bbc.com/news/world-africa-47172020

social change. However, the system was not ready to deliver the needed changes. This situation prompted the military to take control of the country by toppling Haile Selassie's regime in 1974. The military regime, led by Colonel Mengistu Haile Mariam, imposed socialism in Ethiopia, ruling the country until 1991. Sadly enough, the military leadership failed to lead the country to a better future. Then it was toppled by the Ethiopian People's Revolutionary Democratic Front (EPRDF). The current political system is structured as a federal parliamentary republic, where the prime minister is the head of the Ethiopian government.

The current regime is also beset by social unrest and clashes among ethnic groups, and by new claims for self-determination. In general, the country faces a tremendous task of lifting the burden of poverty, and the focus should rest on national unity and the rule of law for development to take roots.

5. The Economy

Ethiopia is a developing country plagued by poverty and inequality. However, in recent years, the country has achieved impressive growth. In 2018, Ethiopia became Africa's fastest growing economy, with 8.5 percent GDP growth rate. Investment in infrastructure and manufacturing contributed to economic growth. In 2016–2017, foreign direct investment grew by 27.6 percent.[13]

The CIA World Factbook highlights the projects Ethiopia is set to accomplish and identifies state-owned economic sectors. "Ongoing infrastructure projects include power production

---

[13] Ethiopia is Africa's fastest-growing economy, 04 May 2018. Retrieved from https://www.weforum.org/agenda/2018/05/ethiopia-africafastest-growing-economy/

and distribution, roads, rails, airports and industrial parks. Key sectors are state-owned, including telecommunications, banking and insurance, and power distribution. Under Ethiopia's constitution, the state owns all land and provides long-term leases to tenants. Title rights in urban areas, particularly Addis Ababa, are poorly regulated, and subject to corruption."[14]

While signs of economic growth are encouraging, Ethiopia is still a poor country. Its GDP for 2019 was estimated at US$96.1 billion. Compared to the world economies, Ethiopia ranks sixty-third in GDP. For 2015, the World Bank estimated the poverty rate at 23.5 percent,[15] meaning that nearly a fourth of Ethiopians lived below poverty line.

5.1 GDP of Ethiopia

Gross domestic product (GDP) measures the total market value of final goods and services produced annually in a country. It is a macroeconomic indicator, used for assessing the overall economic performance of a country and for a comparative approach.

Because GDP is a measure of macroeconomic performance, it does not provide a detailed picture of the changes in the standard of living of the society. Therefore, it is useful to assess social indicator trends, such as life expectancy and access to clean water, healthcare, and education, etc., to capture changes in the standard of living. The next chapter provides analysis, using social indicators, to track poverty and inequality gaps

---

[14] CIA, The World Factbook (February 2020). Retrieved from https://www.cia.gov/library/publications/the-world-factbook/geos/et.html

[15] World Bank Data. Retrieved from: https://data.worldbank.org/indicator/NY.GDP.MKTP.KD.ZG?display=&locations=ET-AE

between the rich and the poor. This current chapter continues the discussion on GDP, per capita GDP, international trade, and the trade balance of Ethiopia.

Table 2 (below) displays Ethiopia's GDP or total output. We can see that the GDP increased from around US$30 billion in 2010 to US$96 billion in 2019. Per capita GDP increased from US$342 in 2010 to US $542 in 2017. Table 3 also captures data on Nominal GDP and Real GDP. Nominal GDP is the GDP that has not been adjusted for inflation, while Real GDP is the GDP that has been adjusted for inflation.

Table 2 GDP of Ethiopia (2010–2019)

Year	$US billion
2019	95.9
2018	84.3
2017	81.8
2016	74.3
2015	64.6
2014	55.6
2013	47.6
2012	43.3
2011	31.9
2010	29.9

Source: World Bank. Retrieved from: https://data.worldbank.org/indicator/NY.GDP.MKTP.CD?locations=ET

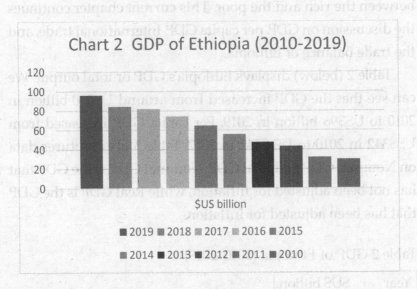

Chart 2 GDP of Ethiopia (2010-2019)

$US billion

■ 2019 ■ 2018 ■ 2017 ■ 2016 ■ 2015

■ 2014 ■ 2013 ■ 2012 ■ 2011 ■ 2010

Chart created by author based on world Bank data.

Table 3 Nominal and real GDP of Ethiopia (2010–2017)

Year	Nominal GDP(BN$)	Real GDP(BN$)	GDP (%) Change	GDP Per Capita
2017	80.5	57.7	10.3	$542
2016	73	52.3	7.6	505
2015	64.5	48.7	10.4	483
2014	55.6	44.1	10.3	449
2013	47.6	39.9	10.6	419
2012	43.3	36.2	8.7	390
2011	31.9	33.2	11.1	369
2010	29.9	29.9	12.5	342

Source: World Bank National and OECD national
accounts data. GDP (current US$) | Data (worldbank.org)

Sectoral Composition of GDP (2010-2019)

The shift in the sectoral composition of the GDP is displayed in Table 4. Between 2010 and 2019, the share of agriculture in GDP decreased from 41% to 34%, and the share of services decreased from 41.8% to 37.1%. Industry's share in GDP increased from 9% to 25%, and the share of manufacturing also increased from 4% to 6%.

Table 4 The share of Economic Sectors in GDP (%)- Ethiopia

Economic Sectors	2010	2019
Agriculture	41	34
Industry	9	25
Manufacturing	4	6
Services	41.8	37.1

Source: World Bank, World Development Indicators. Retrieved from: http://wdi.worldbank.org/table/4.2

Chart 3 The Share of Economic Sectors in GDP (%) -Ethiopia

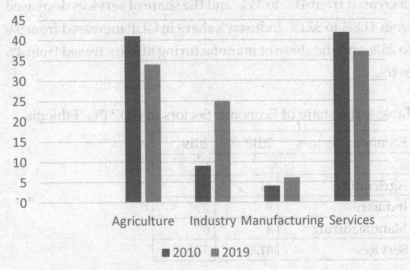

Chart created by author based on World Bank data

6. Trade

"When countries open [up] to trade, they generally benefit because they can sell more, then they can buy more. And trade has a two-way gain."[16] – Jeffrey Sachs, Special Advisor to the UN Secretary-General and former Director of the UN Millennium Project. Paul Krugman also asserts the benefits of international trade for the entire world as a whole, "and especially for poorer nations—growing trade between high-wage and low-wage

---

[16] Colorado Fernandez, Trade and the MDGS: How Trade Can Help Developing Countries Eradicate Poverty. Retrieved from: https://www. un.org/en/chronicle/article/trade-and   -mdgs-how-trade-can-help-developing -countries-eradicate-poverty

countries is a very good thing. Above all, it offers backward economies their best hope of moving up the income ladder."[17] However, it is crucial for developing countries to establish institutions and initiate development policies that would help them to reap the benefits of international trade.

Table 5 Top five products (exports/imports) Ethiopia (2016)

Top Five Products (Exports)	In,000 US$
Coffee, not roasted or decaffeinated	714,836.80
Gold in other semi manufactured form	128,805.73
Dried kidney beans, incl. white pea beans	107,572.82
Fresh, chilled, or frozen goat meat	93,474.20
Dried chickpeas, shelled	67,238.32

Top Five Products (Imports)	in '000 US $
Petroleum oils	1,924,826.08
Palm oil (excl. crude) and liquid fraction	522,509.62

[17] Paul Krugman, *The New York Times* (vol.157, issue 54172), Dec 28, 2007

Prepared, unrecorded media for sound recording	411,934.24
Aircraft	405,312.47
Other fertilizers	361,705.21

World Bank. Retrieved from: https://wits.worldbank.org/CountryProfile/en/Country/ETH/Year/LTST/Summary

Based on the export data for the top five products (for 2016), the share of coffee accounted for 64%, while the export of gold, dried kidney beans, dried peas, and chilled or frozen goat meat comprised 36%. The data corroborates Ethiopia's dependence on monocrop to generate export revenue. Ethiopia's top imports (for 2016) include petroleum oil, palm oil, motor vehicles, aircraft, and fertilizers. Petroleum oil and palm oil accounted for 67% of the total imports.

Ethiopia's Trade Partners

The United States, Saudi Arabia, Germany, Switzerland, and China are Ethiopia's top five trade partners. The U.S. has the largest market share (9.8%), followed by Saudi Arabia, with a market share of 9.7%. Germany ranks third, with a market share of 8.6%. Switzerland and China rank fourth and fifth, with 7.6% and 5.1% of the market shares, respectively.

Table 6 Ethiopia's Trade Partners

Market	Total (US $ Mil)	Partner Share (%)
U.S.	169	9.8
Saudi Arabia	167	9.7
Germany	148	8.6
Switzerland	131	7.6
China	89	5.1

Source: World Integrated Trade Solution (WITS) https://wits.worldbank.org/countrysnapshot/en/ETH

In 2019, Ethiopia's exports accounted for US$7.6 billion, and its imports comprised US $20.0 billion, resulting in a negative trade balance of $12.4 billion (based on World Bank, TCdata360).

7. Summary

Ethiopia is an ancient independent country located in the Horn of Africa, with a land area of 386,102 square miles. The capital city, Addis Ababa, hosts international headquarters, notably, the Economic Commission for Africa (ECA) and the Organization of African Unity (OAU).

Ethiopia is the second most populous country in Africa, and twelfth in the world, with a total population of 114.96 million, 49.7% female and 50.3% male. Youth between the ages of 15 and 24 account for 22% of the total population. The median age is twenty, and life expectancy is sixty-six years. The average fertility rate per woman was 4.73 in the period 2016–2019, with the average rate of population growth estimated at 2.6% per year. Urban population comprises 21% of the total population, and rural population accounts for 79%. The share of urban population is expected to increase with increase in the number of people migrating from rural to urban areas.

In 2018, Ethiopia became the fastest growing economy in Africa with a GDP growth rate of 8.5%. In 2019, the country's GDP was estimated at US$96.1 billion, and the per capita income was estimated at US$857. Ethiopia's major trading partners are the United States, Saudi Arabia, Germany, Switzerland, and China. Foreign trade accounts for 29% of GDP, with a negative trade balance of $12.4 billion. The country's major export (coffee) accounts for 64% of total exports. The path to sustained growth hinges on an economic model based on diversification and inclusive development strategy.

CHAPTER II

Income Distribution, Household Expenditure, Cost of Living, Health, Housing, and Education

1. Introduction

The purpose of this chapter is to address the prevalence of inequality on several fronts. First, the chapter explores income inequality based on comparative data to illustrate the country's global standing. Then, household expenditure differences will be assessed to demonstrate how the poor are neglected. This chapter also examines the impact of inflation on the poor in the context of real-world examples. Analysis of inequality will also take place based on human development index, and Gini coefficient.

Health indicators, such as life expectancy, maternal mortality rate, and physician population ratios; and education indicators, such as student-teacher ratio, and school dropout data will be presented to assess inequalities and provide suggestions for better opportunities and access to quality healthcare and education. The urban housing problem will also be explored to provide suggestions in terms of mitigating the issue.

2. Income Distribution

Ethiopia is among the poorest eleven countries in the world, with a per capita income of $856. Uganda, Guinea-Bissau, Togo, Niger, Congo Democratic Republic, Afghanistan, Mozambique, Central African Republic, Sudan, and Malawi are also included in the list. With Afghanistan as an exception, the bottom ten in the list are African countries. Table 7 (below) shows a huge difference between per capita incomes of the top and the bottom eleven countries.

For all countries included in the table, per capita GDP is reported for 2019. However, for Monaco and Liechtenstein, the 2018 data is reported.

Table 7 Per capita GDP (in US$) (2019) –
Low Income Countries

Ethiopia	856
Uganda	794
Guinea-Bissau	697
Togo	679
Niger	554
DR of Congo	581
Afghanistan	507
Mozambique	504
Central Afr. Republic	468
Sudan	442
Malawi	412

Per capita GDP (in US$) (2019) – Top Eleven Upper Income Countries

Monaco (2018)	185,829
Liechtenstein (2018)	181,403
Luxembourg	114,705
Macao China	84,096
Switzerland	81,994
Ireland	78,661
Norway	75,420
U.S.	65,298
Singapore	65,233
Netherlands	52,331
Sweden	51,615

Source: World Bank. Retrieved from: GDP per capita (current US$) | Data (worldbank.org)

Just comparing the per capita income of Sweden (a mixed-economy country) and Ethiopia, we see that on the average, the per capita income of Sweden is twenty-four times more than the per capita income of Ethiopia based on Purchasing Power Parity (PPP) (at current international $ based on World Bank data). PPP is a "popular macroeconomic analysis metric to compare economic productivity and standards of living between countries ... PPP is an economic theory that compares different countries' currencies through a 'basket of goods' approach" (Investopedia).

In addition to per capita income, the human development index provides valuable insight into the country's status regarding the standard of living of the society. "The Human Development Index (HDI) is a summary measure of average achievement in key dimensions of human development: a long and healthy life, being knowledgeable and having a decent standard of living" (UNDP http://hdr.undp.org/en/content/human-development-index-hdi).

The human development index for Ethiopia (for 2019) was estimated at 0.47, showing a slight improvement from the 2010 index of 0.412 and the 2015 index of 0.453. However, globally, Ethiopia ranked 173rd in the world in terms of social and economic development, based on data trends from 2000 to 2019. Life expectancy at birth is estimated at sixty-six years, with expected years of schooling estimated at nine years. Appendix 1 (pp. 171-179) includes additional information on human development indicators for Ethiopia.

According to the Gini coefficient, a statistical measure of economic inequality, income share held by the fourth 20% (quintile) of Ethiopians declined from 21.3% in 2010 to 20.6% in 2015. However, income share held by the highest 10% increased from 27.4% to 31.4%. Also, income share held by the highest 20% increased from 41.7% to 46.75%. Poverty head count ratio at $1.90 a day declined from 9.10% in 2010 to 7.7% in 2015. For additional information, see Appendix 2 (p. 181).

In the face of income inequality, workers are also not protected from exploitation by international investors. The government's motivation to attract foreign investment prompted the lowest wage for Ethiopian workers employed in the garment industry. CNBC reported that the Ethiopian workers in the garment industry earn the lowest monthly wage, equivalent to US$26. Turkish workers, with a monthly wage of US$340, earn thirteen times the monthly wage of Ethiopian workers in the same industry. A Chinese worker earns US$326, which is 12.5 times the monthly wage of an Ethiopian worker. And a Kenyan, with a monthly wage of US$207, earns almost eight times the monthly wage of an Ethiopian worker in the same industry.[18]

Chart 4 Where Pay is Lowest for Cheap Clothing Production

Where Is Lowest For Cheap Clothing Production
Monthly minimum wage in the global garment industry in 2018 (selected countries)

Country	Monthly minimum wage
Turkey	$340
China	$326
Thailand	$309
Indonesia	$280
Malaysia	$267
South Africa	$244
Kenya	$207
Cambodia	$182
Vietnam	$180
Lesotho	$146
Laos	$128
Bangladesh	$95
Myanmar	$95
Ethiopia	$26

©①= @StatistaCharts   Source: NYU Stern Center for Business and Human Rights   **statista**⚊

3. Household Expenditure

The household consumer expenditure survey for Ethiopia (2015–2016) highlights a huge expenditure gap between rich and poor Ethiopians. According to Table 8 (below) the first group includes 20% of households with the lowest annual per capita expenditures of less than or equal to 5379.81 Birr, equivalent to US$131. On the other hand, the last group, 20% of households,

---

[18] Ethiopia's garment workers are world's lowest paid. Retrieved from: https://www.cnbc.com/2019/05/07/report-ethiopias-garment-workers-are-worlds-lowest-paid.html

**Note: 1 US dollar = 41.88 Ethiopian Birr, as of April 27, 2021

spends equal to or greater than 15,110.22 Birr, equivalent to US$367, a 180% increase compared to expenditures by the first 20% of households. And when cost of living increases, the purchasing power of consumers decreases, disproportionately affecting the poor.

Table 8 Household Expenditure Survey (2015–2016)

Quintiles	% HHS	HH Expenditure (per capita in Birr) (lower limit)	(upper limit
I	20		< or =5,379.81
II	20	5,379.81	7,688.06
II	20	7,688.11	10,122.00
IV	20	10,123.36	15,109.20
V	20	> or =15,110.22	

Source: Central Statistical Agency of Ethiopia, p.16
http://www.statsethiopia.gov.et/wp-content/uploads/2019/06/Househol d-Consumption-Expenditure- Survey-2016.pdf
Note: At 2015–2016, national average prices not spatially adjusted for regional differences

The above survey shows a big expenditure gap between low income and upper income households. Poor Ethiopians find it a daunting task to put food on the table, especially in a situation where food prices are skyrocketing. According to Trading Economics, "cost of food in Ethiopia increased 25.9 percent in April of 2020 over the same month in the previous year."[19] Ethiopians are also experiencing hunger. The World

---

[19] Trading Economics. Retrieved from: tradingeconomics.com/ethiopia/ unemployment-rate

Food Program projected that by 2020, "8 million Ethiopians [would] need food assistance." [20]

Why is Ethiopia a victim of famine?

Internal conflict or unrest, and inadequate government response are the reasons for persistence of famine in Ethiopia. The famine of 1983-1985, which claimed the lives of 1 million Ethiopians,[21] shocked the world community.

In the context of the current situation, food insecurity will continue in Ethiopia, and the tensions between ethnic dominant groups may also continue unabated, unless sweeping measures are taken to resolve the problems. Until then, Ethiopians will find ways to emigrate to a better place. The PEW Research documented that Ethiopians were among the top three African countries migrating to the U.S. in 2015.[22]

According to *Migration and Remittances Fact Book*, "it is estimated that total remittances have exceeded $601 billion. Of that amount, developing countries are estimated to receive about $441 billion, nearly three times the amount of official development assistance. The true size of remittances, including unrecorded flows through formal and informal channels, is believed to be significantly larger."[23]

Table 9 (below) includes remittances sent to Ethiopia between

---

[20] UN, World Food Program. Retrieved from: https://www.wfp.org/countries/ethiopia

[21] See: An Africa Watch Report, Sept 1991. Retrieved from: https://www.hrw.org/sites/default/files/reprts/Ethiopia919.pdf

[22] PEW Research Center. February 14, 2017. African immigrant population in U.S. steadily climbs | Pew Research Center

[23] The World Bank, *Migration and Remittances Fact Book, 2016* (3rd ed.)

2015 and 2019. And when considering the total remittances sent to Ethiopia during 2015 and 2019, remittances sent in 2015 account for 34% (the highest share), and remittances sent in 2017 account for 12% (the lowest share).

Table 9 Remittances sent to Ethiopia.

Year	Million US$
2015	1,087
2016	772
2017	393
2018	436
2019	531

Chart 5 Remittances sent to Ethiopia

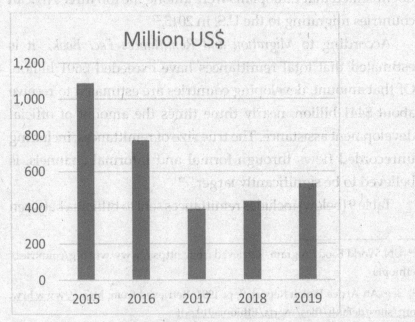

Source: World Bank, Migration & Remittance Data, updated April 2020

"A remittance is a payment of money that is transferred to another party. Broadly speaking, any payment of an invoice or a bill can be called a remittance. However, the term is most often used nowadays to describe a sum of money sent by someone working abroad to his or her family back home" (Investopedia).

The Pew Research Center highlights the contribution of remittances from abroad as "major economic assets for developing countries"[24] It is evident that remittances will be life saving for poor people.[25] They need the money for the purchase of food and other necessities. And when money is spent, it stimulates the economy, money circulation increases, and banks or financial intermediaries participate by facilitating currency exchange between, say, the US dollar and the Ethiopian Birr. As a result, banks' reserves of hard currencies increase.

Access to foreign currency, such as the US dollar and the euro, enhances international trade and stimulates the economy. However, according to the World Bank's methodology of ranking business climate, Ethiopia is ranked 159th out of 190 countries. Therefore, the regulatory environment is not conducive enough to attract investment in Ethiopia.[26] Despite this shortcoming, the Chinese investment, and the proliferation of industrial zones in Ethiopia are encouraging signs provided that the government enforces better working conditions and living wage.

---

[24] The PEW Research Center (Jan 29, 2018). Retrieved from: Remittances can be big economic assets for countries | Pew Research Center

[25] Due to the covid-19 pandemic, the World Bank predicts sharpest declines in remittances. For Sub-Saharan Africa, the flow of remittance is estimated to decline by 23 percent. (World Bank, April 22, 2020)

[26] The World Bank, *Doing Business 2020*. Retrieved from: https://www.doingbusiness.org/en/doingbusiness

4. Wage and Cost of Living

4.1 Wage

The International Labor Organization's (ILO) global report (2016-2017) highlights the prevalence of wage inequality in many countries, and the impact of inequality on the society and the economy. The report also addresses "gender wage inequality, greater household income inequality and declining labor shares." According to gender inequality index, Ethiopia ranks 129th in the world. The ILO reports that "just 10 percent of workers receive nearly half of global pay" (ILO, July 4, 2019).

The ILO also estimates that in 2020, 20% of working Ethiopian women twenty-five years of age and more, and 22% of working men in the same age bracket, earn below US$1.90 per day in purchasing power parity (PPP).[27] The gap between the minimum wage and the living wage is very wide. The ILO report on minimum wage for 2018 reflects a huge gap between the top ten countries and developing countries, including Ethiopia. The average minimum wage ($1,897) for the top ten countries (Luxembourg, Australia, New Zealand, Ireland, Netherlands, Belgium, France, Germany, United Kingdom, and New Caledonia) is almost 73 times the monthly wage ($26) of Ethiopian workers in the garment factory, based on purchasing power parity (PPP).[28]

---

[27] ILO, Statistics on Wages, ILOSTAT 2020 estimate

[28] ILO STAT https://ilostat.ilo.org/topics/wages/

4.2 Cost of Living

"The Consumer Price Index (CPI) is a measure of the average change over time in the prices paid by urban consumers for a market basket of consumer goods and services" (US Bureau of Statistics). The CPI basket includes food and beverages, housing, apparel, transportation, health, recreation, education, restaurants and hotels, and miscellaneous goods and services.

Table 10 (below) displays the inflation rates for Ethiopia for the periods, 2015 to 2019. According to the data, in a span of four years (2015 to 2019) consumer prices have increased from 9.57% to 15.84%, a net increase of 6.27%. This means that for poor people, it is a burden to sustain life when their purchasing power is diminished due to inflationary pressure in the economy. Inflation also erodes consumer confidence about the economy.

Table 10 Ethiopia-Inflation Rate (2015–2019)

(annual %) Year	Inflation (%)
2019	15.84
2018	13.83
2017	10.68
2016	6.63
2015	9.57

World Bank Inflation, consumer prices (annual %) | Data (worldbank.org)

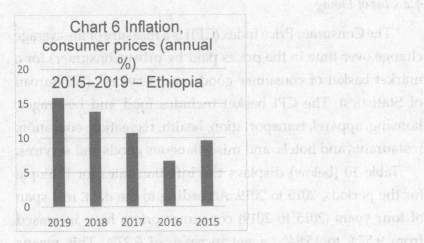

Chart 6 Inflation, consumer prices (annual %) 2015–2019 – Ethiopia

Chart created by author based on data from the World Bank.

In Ethiopia, expenditures on food and non-alcoholic beverages comprised 53%, and non-food expenditures accounted for 43%, out of which expenditures on housing, water, electricity, gas, and other fuels accounted for 16.34% (Central Statistical Agency of Ethiopia, 2017).

The food consumption expenditure pattern reported for Ethiopia shows a trend like the other developing countries. Among the countries that spend the most on food, Nigeria is on top of the list. Table 11 (below) shows nine countries spending the most on food.[29]

Engel's law[30] reflects the pattern of food expenditure in developing economies. This means that poor households spend

---

[29] World Economic Forum, Dec.07, 2016. Retrieved from: https://www.weforum.org/agenda/2016/12/this-map-shows-how-much-each-country-spends-on-food/

[30] For details, see Benjamin S. Loeb, "Use of Engel's Laws as a basis for predicting consumer expenditures," in *Journal of Marketing*, vol. 20 Issue 1, July,1955.

most of their budget on food. On the other hand, rich households spend more money on nonedible items and relatively less money on food.

Consumption patterns have strong linkages with income. Andreas Chai[31] discusses consumption patterns as income grows, and the implication of the trend on industrial composition, on demographic, geographic, and social factors.

Table 11 Countries spending the most on food (2015)

	% of consumption expenditure on food
Azerbaijan	40.1
Guatemala	40.6
Pakistan	40.9
Philippines	41.9
Algeria	42.5
Kazakhstan	43
Cameroon	45.
Kenya	46.7
Nigeria	56.4

Source: World Economic Forum
World Economic Forum (weforum.org)

In 2015, eight countries spent less than 10% of their household income on food. From the group (listed in Table 12), consumers in the United States spent 6.4% of their earnings on food, the lowest food expenditure.

---

[31] Andreas Chai, Household consumption patterns and the sectoral composition of growing economies: A review of the interlinkages, UNIDOO, Vienna, 2018, p. 3 Retrieved from: https://www.unido.org/api/opentext/documents/download/10166980/unido-file-10166980

Table 12 Countries spending the least on food (2015)

	Exp (%)
United States	6.4
Singapore	6.7
United Kingdom	8.2
Switzerland	8.7
Canada	9.1
Ireland	9.6
Australia	9.8
Austria	9.9

Source: World Economic Forum (Dec. 7, 2016)

4.2.1 Food Inflation

In Ethiopia, food prices increased from 10.7% in January 2019, to 22% in January 2020, and then to 25.9% in April 2020. Among African countries, where food is expensive, Zimbabwe ranks first place, South Sudan in second place, Liberia in third place, and Ethiopia in fourth place. Globally, Ethiopia ranks sixth in food inflation (Trading Economics, 2020). According to the World Bank, "increased food prices negatively affect income, nutrition and health of poor consumers."[32] In other words, increased food prices aggravate poverty in a society that struggles to put food on the table every day.

The information on wages and price trends indicates that the Ethiopian economy is experiencing inflationary pressure.

[32] The World Bank, September 13, 2012. Retrieved from: https://www.worldbank.org/en/news/feature/2012/09/13/america_latina_crisis_precio_alimentos

Inflation takes away the purchasing power of money. Low wage earners and the poor are highly affected by inflation.

Globally, in the list of countries affected by inflation, Venezuela ranks first, with 2299% inflation rate, and Zimbabwe ranks second, with 737% inflation rate. From top down, Ethiopia (with 22.5% inflation rate) is eleventh.[33]

I will briefly address the impact of inflation on three countries: Egypt, Zimbabwe, and Venezuela. Food price inflation contributed to the crisis in Egypt. According to the Guardian, "when grain prices spiked in 2007–2008, Egypt's bread prices rose 37%. With unemployment rising as well, more people depended on subsidized bread—but the government did not make any more food available. Egypt's annual food price inflation continued and had hit 18.9% before the fall of President Mubarak."[34]

Inflation in Zimbabwe triggered food shortages. According to Bloomberg, "bankers_joined nurses, doctors and other health-care professionals demanding to be paid in U.S. dollars to cushion themselves against soaring inflation and the depreciating local currency."[35] The hyperinflation of Venezuela forced 4.5 million Venezuelans to leave their country "blighted

[33] Trading Economics 2020, data reference for Venezuela is May 2020, for Zimbabwe, June 2020, and for Ethiopia, June 2020). Retrieved from: https://tradingeconomics.com/country-list/inflation-rate

[34] *The Guardian* (issued on July 16, 2011). Retrieved from https://www.theguardian.com/lifeandstyle/2011/jul/17/bread-food-arab-spring

[35] *Bloomberg*, July 14, 2020. Retrieved from https://www.bloomberg.com/news/articles/2020-07-14/zimbabwe-continues-its-march-back-to-hyperinflation

by unemployment, collapsing utilities, a defunct healthcare system and severe food shortages."[36]

5. Housing

Rapid urban population growth in sub-Saharan Africa has aggravated the housing shortage. According to the World Bank, "Sub-Saharan Africa is experiencing rapid urbanization as well as a growing slum population." The World Bank also reports that in most of the African nations, urbanization has not been accompanied by industrial growth. Table 13 shows selected sub-Saharan African countries experiencing high annual urban population growth. Ethiopia ranks third, with urban population growth rate of 4.8%. Burundi, with 5.7%, and Burkina Faso with 4.9%, rank first and second, respectively.

Table 13 - Urban Population Growth
(Selected Sub-Saharan Africa Countries)

Country	Year	%
Angola	2019	4.2
Nigeria	2019	4.2
Zambia	2019	4.2
Ethiopia	2019	4.8
Burkina Faso	2019	4.9
Burundi	2019	5.7

Source: World Bank, Urban population growth (annual %) | Data (worldbank.org)

---

[36] *The Guardian*, July 30, 2020. https://www.theguardian.com/global-development/2020/jul/30/a-dollar-for-sex-venezuelas-women-tricked-and-trafficked

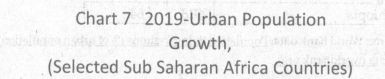

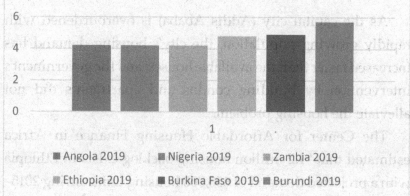

Chat created by author based on World Bank data.

Urban population growth in Ethiopia is accompanied by growth in slums. Table 14 shows the five countries with significant share of their urban populations living in slums. Central African Republic, with 95% of its urban population living in slums, ranks number one, and Ethiopia is in fifth place, with 64% of its urban residents living in slums.

Table 14 Percent of Urban Population Living in Slums

Country	Year	%
South Sudan	2018	91
Central African Republic	2018	95
Chad	2018	87

| Afghanistan | 2018 | 71 |
| Ethiopia | 2018 | 64 |

Source: World Bank data, Population living in slums (% of urban population) | Data (worldbank.org).

As the capital city (Addis Ababa) is overburdened with rapidly growing population, the city's housing demand has increased faster than the available houses, and the government's intervention by building condos and apartments did not alleviate the housing problem.

The Center for Affordable Housing Finance in Africa estimated that "1.2 million housing backlog exists in Ethiopia with a projected demand of 655,800 housing units during 2015–2025, by far exceeding the estimated annual supply of housing of about 165,000 units nation-wide between 2007/2008 and 2013/2014."[37] The World Bank group reports that "government-led housing supply—mainly in the form of the IHDP—is unable to meet demand, is fiscally unsustainable, and is not affordable for the bottom 40% of the population."[38] The urban poor are also excluded from the mortgage market because the market caters to wealthy individuals and to those who provide collaterals.

Table 15 (below) shows that most households in lower consumption quintiles (Q1, Q2) occupy informally constructed houses, while households in higher consumption quintiles (Q4, Q5) occupy cooperative, formal, or IHDP housing.

---

[37] Center for Affordable Housing Finance in Africa (CAHF) (2019) http://housingfinanceafrica.org/

[38] World Bank Group, *Urban Land Supply and Affordable Housing Study Synthesis Report*, 7.

Table 15 Proportion of Households by Quintile

Household Consumption	Coop Housing	Formally Constructed Housing	IHDP
Quintiles			
Q1 (lowest)	5.5	12.4	8.9
Q2	7.7	12.8	11.6
Q3	15.6	16.7	18.4
Q4	22.4	21.4	23.6
Q5 (highest)	47.8	36.6	37.6

Source: Unlocking Ethiopia's Urban Land and Housing Markets (Synthesis Report) (worldbank.org).

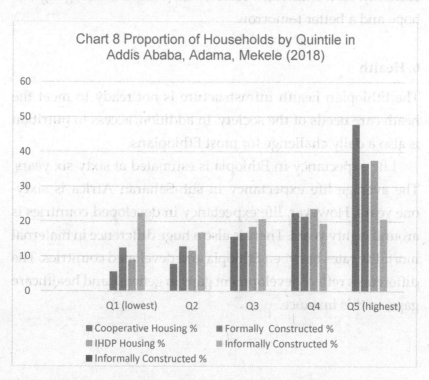

Chart 8 Proportion of Households by Quintile in Addis Ababa, Adama, Mekele (2018)

Source: World Bank: Unlocking Ethiopia's Urban Land and Housing Market.
IHDP = Integrated Housing Development Plan

How can the problem be mitigated?

The government should cater to the poor by building affordable houses. At the same time, the government should focus its efforts on expanding or establishing cities in rural areas to stave off rural to urban migration.

Access to affordable housing has multidimensional benefits. Individuals and families living in affordable housing get satisfaction from the safety and security the house provides. When families know that they can afford to pay rent, and when they have extra income to spend on food, clothing, and transportation, their expenditures in turn stimulate the economy. In a nutshell, access to affordable housing signals hope and a better tomorrow.

6. Health

The Ethiopian health infrastructure is not ready to meet the heath care needs of the society. In addition, access to nutrition is also a daily challenge for most Ethiopians.

Life expectancy in Ethiopia is estimated at sixty-six years. The average life expectancy in sub-Saharan Africa is sixty-one years. However, life expectancy in developed countries is around eighty years. There is also a huge difference in maternal mortality rates between Ethiopia and developed countries. The differences reflect development gaps in general, and healthcare gaps, in this instance.

Table 16 Life Expectancy (2018)

Country	Life Expectancy (Years)
Ethiopia	66
U.S.A.	79
Germany	80
Sweden	83
Italy	83

Source: World Bank data, https://data.worldbank.org/indicator/SP.DYN.

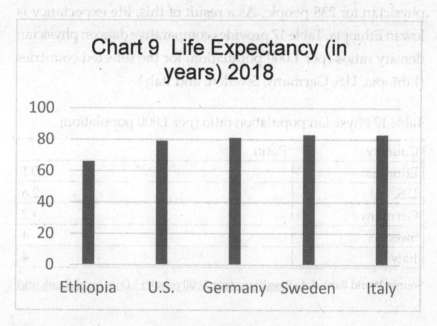

Chart created by author, based on World Bank data.

People in developed countries have access to quality healthcare and better nutrition and education, while poor people in Ethiopia, and other developing countries are remotely connected to quality healthcare and better nutrition.

Physician-to-population ratio also explains the differences in healthcare access between the rich and the poor economies.

For comparison, I have selected four countries that are industrialized and Ethiopia (a developing country) to assess the gap between physician-to-population ratios (per 1000 population).

Table 17 shows that that the physician population ratio is 0.1 for Ethiopia, 2.6 for the United States, 4.2 for Germany, 4 for Sweden, and 4 for Italy. This means that in Ethiopia there is one physician for 10,000 people, while in Germany there is one physician for 238 people. As a result of this, life expectancy is low in Ethiopia. Table 17 provides comparative data on physician density ratios (per 1,000 population) for the selected countries (Ethiopia, U.S, Germany, Sweden, and Italy).

Table 17 Physician population ratio (per 1,000 population)

Country	Ratio
Ethiopia	0.1
U.S.	2.6
Germany	4.2
Sweden	4
Italy	4

Source: World Bank data Physicians (per 1,000 people) | Data (worldbank.org).

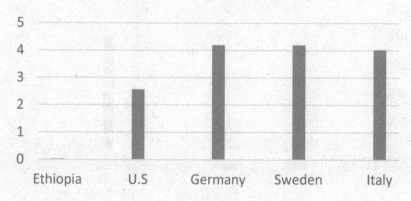

Chart 10 Physician Population Density (per 1000 population)

Chart created by author based on World Bank data.

Note: The physician density ratio for Ethiopia and Italy is for year 2018, for Germany and the U.S., the ratio is for 2017, and for Sweden, the ratio is for 2016.

The maternal mortality rate also is exceedingly high in Ethiopia (401 deaths per 100,000 live births in 2017). Italy experienced the lowest maternal mortality rate from the group, with 2 deaths per 100,000 live births.

Table 18 Maternal Mortality Ratio (per 100,000 births)

Country	Ratio
Sweden	4
U.S.	19
Germany	7
Italy	2
Ethiopia	401

Source: World Bank, https://data.worldbank Maternal mortality ratio (modeled estimate, per 100,000 live births) | Data (worldbank.org).

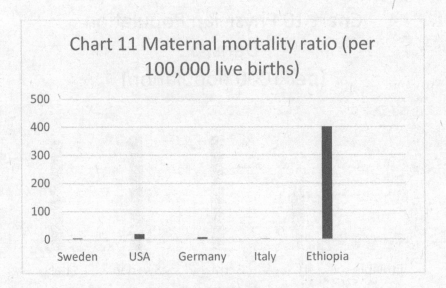

Chart created by author based on World Bank data.

The preceding information highlights the prevalence of health inequality between developed and developing countries. Health inequality is also pervasive between poor and rich people in Ethiopia.

Michael Jetter addresses the link between income levels and life expectancy, suggesting "that income levels seem to be the strongest factor in raising life expectancy across the globe,"[39] and asserts that "promoting economic growth is potentially a powerful tool to guarantee healthy and long lives."[40]

To bridge health inequality, the Ethiopian government should mobilize resources to expand healthcare for the poor. A healthy society implies a vibrant economy. In the final analysis,

---

[39] Michael Jetter. The Intimate Link Between Income Levels and Life Expectancy: "Global Evidence from 213 Years", in *Social Science Quarterly*, June 1, 2019.

[40] Jetter, "Global Evidence."

however, the preconditions for achieving a healthy society and a vibrant economy rest on good governance.

7. Education

Education provides interwoven multidimensional benefits ranging from poverty reduction to improved nutrition, health, and well-being, to inequality reduction, environmental protection, and peaceful, just, and inclusive societies. The Global Partnership for Education[41] highlights the benefits of education as follows:

a. 420 million people would be lifted out of poverty with a secondary education,
b. a child whose mother can read is 50% more likely to live past the age of 5, and
c. one additional year of school can increase a woman's earnings by up to 20 percent.

UNICEF reports that "more than half of children remain excluded from pre-primary education in Ethiopia, despite impressive gains made in increasing enrollment."[42]

To redress the problem, UNICEF strongly urges the Ethiopian government to increase spending on pre-primary education in neglected areas of the country. If the problem is

---

[41] Global Partnership for Education. Retrieved from: https://www.globalpartnership.org/benefits-of-education.

[42] UNICEF (April 9, 2020). Retrieved from: https://www.unicef.org/ethiopia/press-releases/more-half-children-remain-excluded-pre-primary-education-ethiopia-despite-impressive.

not tackled, children's potential will be stymied, and their full development and growth will be hampered.

The ensuing paragraphs highlight Ethiopia's standing in primary, secondary, and postsecondary school enrollments (based on data extracted from Index Mundi).

In primary school enrollment, Ethiopia ranked 110th in the world and 23rd in Africa in 2015. In secondary school enrollment for male students, Ethiopia ranked 160th in the world and 32nd in Africa. In female student enrollment in secondary school, Ethiopia ranked 175th in the world and 32nd in Africa. In postsecondary school enrollment, Ethiopia ranked 134th in the world and 16th in Africa. For tertiary school enrollment, Ethiopia ranked 140th in the world for male students and 25th in Africa; and for female students, the country ranked 157th in the world and 32nd in Africa. In adult literacy, Ethiopia ranked 144th in the world and 38th in Africa.

Table 19 (below) includes student-teacher ratio for primary school. The ratio for Ethiopia is 55 or one teacher for fifty-five students. This means that primary schools in Ethiopia are underfunded.

Table 19 Student-Teacher Ratio (Primary)

Developing Countries	Year	Ratio
Bangladesh	2018	30
Afghanistan	2018	49
Ethiopia	2011	55
Chad	2016	57

Developed Countries		
Austria	2017	10
Switzerland	2017	10
Sweden	2017	12
Germany	2017	12

Source: World Bank, Pupil-teacher ratio, primary | Data (worldbank.org).

The average student-teacher ratio for the selected developed countries is eleven. This means that a teacher in a developed country spends more time helping students. Therefore, the quality of education will not be compromised. The secondary and upper-secondary school student-teacher ratios for developing and developed countries also show a big difference. The ratios are high for developing countries, including Ethiopia, and low for developed countries. Again, it means that secondary schools in the selected developing countries are underfunded, thereby affecting the quality of education.

Table 20 Student-Teacher Ratio (Secondary)

Developing Countries	Year	Ratio
Chad	2016	27
Afghanistan	2018	34
Bangladesh	2018	35
Ethiopia	2012	40
Developed Countries		
Austria	2017	9
Belgium	2017	9
Norway	2017	9
Germany	2017	12

Source: World Bank Pupil-teacher ratio, secondary | Data (worldbank.org).

Table 21 Student-Teacher Ratio (Upper Secondary)

Developing Countries	Year	Ratio
Angola	2016	22
Bangladesh	2018	29
Afghanistan	2018	33
Ethiopia	2015	44
Developed Countries		
Norway	2017	9
Switzerland	2017	11
France	2013	11
Denmark	2014	12

Source: World Bank, Pupil-teacher ratio, upper secondary | Data (worldbank.org).

Having discussed school enrollment and student-teacher ratios, it is important to assess school completion rate in Ethiopia. Table 22 displays primary school completion rate for selected developed and developing countries, including Ethiopia. The data shows that primary school completion rate (on average) for Norway, the United Kingdom, and the United States is one hundred percent. However, for the developing countries (Ethiopia, Niger, and Equatorial Guinea), the primary school completion rate ranges from 40 percent to 60 percent. For Ethiopia, the completion rate is 54 percent.

A host of factors explain the reasons why school completion rates are very low in developing countries. The time it takes to commute long distance from home to school, the overcrowded class size, and the quality of instruction influence school completion rate. To mitigate this issue, it is recommended to expand existing schools and build new learning facilities closer to the communities where the students live. It is also important to train and employ qualified teachers.

Table 22 Primary School Completion Rate, Total (% of relevant age group)

Developed Countries	
Norway (2018)	99
U.K. (2018)	101
U.S. (2018)	100
Developing Countries	
Ethiopia (2015)	54
Niger (2019)	62
Equatorial Guinea (2015)	41

Source: Primary completion rate, total (% of relevant age group) | Data (worldbank.org)
UNESCO Institute for Statistics (uis.unesco.org). Data as of September 2020.

The secondary school enrollment data for the selected developed and developing countries is included in table 23 (below). The enrollment rate for the developed countries (Norway, United Kingdom and the Unites States) ranges from 92 to 97 percent. For the developing countries (Ethiopia, Niger, and Mali), the enrollment rate ranges from 20 to 31 percent. This means that developing countries need to invest in secondary education. Investment in education fosters economic growth and prepares the society to participate in nation-building activities.

Table 23 School Enrollment, Secondary (% net)

Developed Countries	
Norway (2017)	96
U.K. (2017)	97
U.S. (2017)	92
Developing Countries	
Ethiopia (2015)	31
Niger (2017)	20
Mali (2018)	27

Source: School enrollment, secondary (% net) | Data (worldbank.org).
UNESCO Institute for Statistics (uis.unesco.org). Data as of February 2020.

"Net enrollment rate is the ratio of children of official school age who are enrolled in school to the population of the corresponding official school age. Secondary education completes the provision of basic education that began at the primary level, and aims at laying the foundations for lifelong learning and human development, by offering more subject- or skill-oriented instruction using more specialized teachers" (World Bank).

Table 24 (below) includes data for selected developed and developing countries regarding the percentage of primary school–age children out of school. For the developed countries (Norway, United Kingdom, and the United States), between zero and one percent of primary school age children are out of school. For the developing countries (Ethiopia, Niger, and Equatorial Guinea), between 18 and 55 percent (female) and between 11 and 56 percent (male) primary school–age children are out of school. Again, developing countries need to provide access to primary education.

Table 24 Children Out of School (% of primary school age)

Developed Countries	Female	Male
Norway (2018)	0	0
U.K. (2018)	1	1
U.S. (2018)	1	1
Developing Countries		
Ethiopia (2015)	18	11
Niger (2019)	45	37
Equatorial Guinea (2015)	55	56

Source: Children out of school, female (% of female primary school age) | Data (worldbank.org)
https://data.worldbank.org/indicator/SE.PRM.UNER.MA.ZS.
Institute for Statistics (uis.unesco.org). Data as of September.

The prevalence of educational inequality suggests that it is high time to invest in education and provide better opportunities for children and the society. Access to quality education bridges the inequality gap and fosters economic and social progress.

8. Summary

Ethiopia is among the poorest eleven countries in the world, with a per capita income of $856. Income held by the fourth 20% of Ethiopians declined from 21.3% in 2010 to 20.6% in 2015. On the contrary, income held by the highest 20% increased from 41.7% to 46.7% during the same period. Poverty head count ratio at $1.90 a day declined from 9.10% in 2010 to 7.7% in 2015. Food inflation increased to 25.9% during the month of April 2020. Ethiopia ranks sixth in the world in food inflation. Venezuela and Zimbabwe rank first and second, respectively.

The annual demand for housing (655,800 units) by far exceeds the housing supply of 165,000 units. This housing shortage excludes the urban poor because the market caters to wealthy individuals and to those who provide collaterals.

For Ethiopians, life expectancy is sixty-six years. The average life expectancy in sub-Saharan Africa is sixty-one years. Societies in developed countries live longer, with a life expectancy of eighty years. Maternal mortality rate (per 100,000 live births) for Ethiopia is 400, while it is 2 in Italy, 4 in Sweden, and 7 in Germany. In Ethiopia, there is one physician for 10,000 people, while in Germany there is one physician for about 238 people.

In primary school enrollment, Ethiopia ranks 110th, and in adult literacy, it ranks 157th in the world. There is one teacher for fifty-five students in primary schools, which implies that primary schools in Ethiopia are underfunded. On the other hand, for developed countries, there is one teacher for eleven students. This means that a teacher in a developed country has ample opportunity to monitor the performance of students and provide individualized assistance.

It is important to underline the connection between housing, healthcare, and education. Affordable housing provides safety, peace of mind. and physical health. And the health of a society influences productivity. Education also translates into health outcomes. "A child whose mother can read is 50% more likely to live past the age of 5" (UNICEF).

it is important to underline the connection between housing, healthcare and education. Affordable housing provides stepping stones to better healthcare outcomes as well as positive influences productivity. Education also translates into health outcomes. A child whose mother can read is 50% more likely to live past the age of

CHAPTER III

The Development Strategies of Ethiopia (1960 to 2020)

1. Introduction

This chapter provides a review of Ethiopia's development strategies that have taken place between 1960 and 2020. Starting with the First Five-Year Development Plan (1957–1961), which represented a first-stage program in the development of a modern economy in Ethiopia, the discussion evolves through the decades, covering the development programs of the 1970s, 1980s, and 1990s through 2020. This chapter also explores the reasons why poverty still looms large and provides the springboard for recommendations aimed at curbing poverty.

2. The Development Strategies between 1960s and the 1970s

The development attempts between 1960 and 1974 were designed with the objective of breaking away from poverty. Investment priorities focused on infrastructure, industry, and agriculture.[43] This development approach mirrored the development doctrines of the 1950s,[44] where growth was primarily associated with capital accumulation. However, the achievement of the plan was low, and its impact on agricultural production was also minimum. Against this shortfall, the Second Five-Year Development Plan (1963–1968) resorted to an investment program to speed up the expansion of growth sectors, with more emphasis on industry.

The plan's requirement of 500,000 additional jobs in the modern sector also prompted the need for conducting manpower training.[45] The Third Five-Year Plan (1968–1973) was then rolled out to: a) achieve the overall economic growth rate of 6 percent per year, b) improve the standard of living of the society, c) expand educational opportunities and lay the foundation for future growth, and d) foster regional development (development of river basins, agricultural settlement and resettlement policy, the Setit Humera Region, and Regional Livestock Projects).

The plan was based on monetary investment in the amount of $2.865 million,[46] out of which the money allocated

[43] Second Five-Year Development Plan (1963–1967), (Berhanenna Selam Printing Press, Addis Ababa, Oct 1962), 39–40. Note: "The First Five-Year Development plan represented a first-stage program in the development of a modern economy in Ethiopia."

[44] John M Cohen, *Integrated Rural Development* (The Ethiopian Experience and The Debate), (Motala, 1987), 41.

[45] See Eli Ginzberg and Herbert A. Smith, A Manpower strategy for Ethiopia Addis Ababahttps://www.worldometers.info/world-population/ethiopia-population/, July 1966

[46] Third Five-Year Development Plan of Ethiopia (1968–1973), Berhanenna Selam Printing Press, Addis Ababa, Ethiopia, 50.

for housing, transport and communications, manufacturing and handicrafts, agriculture, forestry, and fishing accounted for 71 percent of the total investment. On the other hand, the monetary investment in health and education accounted for 1.4% and 3.8%, respectively. The manpower requirement of the plan was estimated at 115,000.[47] The breakdown is included in Table 25.

Table 25 Manpower Requirement by Sectors

Sector	Employment
Agriculture	2,470
Mining	280
Manufacturing	36,600
Building & Construction	6,570
Electricity	920
Transport & Communication	13,420
Commerce, banking, etc.	27,350
Education services	12,500
Health services	6,500
Public Admin	8,340
Total	114,950

Source: Third Five-Year Development Plan, 1968–1973.

Note: High level manpower includes professional and technical personnel with four or more years of university education. Intermediate or middle level manpower represents those

---

[47] Third Five-Year Development Plan, 83.

DR. ASSEFA MULUNEH

completing schooling of one to three years beyond secondary education. Skilled workers are those who have completed eighth grade plus one to three years of additional training.[48]

The plan highlighted the skilled manpower shortages of the country. However, it was not possible to quantify the impact of the shortages on the various economic sectors. And the modern sector in the 1960s was too small to generate significant jobs as planned. Therefore, the government promoted a tax holiday to attract imports of capital goods and foster the growth of the modern sector. Agriculture was also underdeveloped due to primitive farming practices. Investment in agriculture was just 16% during the plan period. As a result, average agricultural growth rate did not exceed 2% per year, which was less than the population growth rate of 2.3%.[49] This low growth was reflected by the low per capita GNP (US$56) in the 1960s.[50]

The 1970s witnessed unrest and regime change in Ethiopia. Emperor Haile Selassie's regime was taken over by the military junta, and the transition to socialism created unrest at the time. However, economic development plans continued with the establishment of the Office of the National Committee for Central Planning (ONCCP) in 1979.

---

[48] Third Five-Year Development Plan, 83.

[49] Worldometer. Retrieved from https://www.worldometers.info/world population/ethiopia-population/

[50] Cohen, Integrated Rural Development, 40.

3. The Development Strategy of the 1980s

The development strategy of the 1980s was based on central planning. Four annual- development plans were initiated in the 1980s with the following objectives: a) to ensure the availability of sufficient supply of goods and services to the society, and b) to begin the eradication of deep-seated social problems such as unemployment, illiteracy, etc.[51] Then the Ten-Year Perspective Plan (TYPP) of the country (1983/84–1993/94) was released. The objective of the plan was to bring about improvements in basic social and economic problems and build a strong foundation for uninterrupted growth. The TYPP focused on achieving the overall GDP growth rate of 6.5%. Agriculture was expected to expand by 4.3%, industry by 10.8%, and services by 6.9%. Saving was expected to grow by 23.6% and investment by 16.8%.

Achieving these targets required mobilizing domestic and foreign financial resources. Regarding domestic resources, "public sector institutions as a whole and especially the central government, municipalities, the banking and insurance system, and non-financial public corporations were expected to play the major role."[52] Additionally, public contribution was aimed at facilitating the construction of rural roads, irrigation, and the digging of water wells, for the afforestation and reforestation; and for soil and water conservation programs. However, the domestic savings fell short of the resources required by the TYPP.

---

[51] See Development Campaign Plans II and III (Amharic ed.), Addis Ababa, 1980 and 1981.

[52] ONCCP, TYPP, 49.

Table 26 Cumulative Domestic Savings by Source (1984/85-1993/94)

Source	Million Birr	% of total
Public Sector	9999.1	43.1
Central Govt	3109.6	13.4
Municipalities	727	3.1
Public Enterprise	6162.5	26.6
Private Enterprise Cooperatives & Households	13,200.90	56.9
Urban	6700.2	28.9
Rural	6500.7	28
Total	23,200.00	100

Source: ONCCP, TYPP, 49

Within the broad development objectives of the TYPP, employment strategies focused on generating new job opportunities and increasing labor productivity. However, the implementation of the five-year plan (of the TYPP) demonstrated many shortfalls. In the first place, agriculture, the mainstay of the economy, suffered a series of droughts, reaching the apex in 1985. In the period 1983–1988, agricultural output declined by 3.24%, and gross domestic saving also declined by 3.58%. The periods covering 1974–1988 saw declines in agricultural output of 0.27%. GDP grew by 0.21% during 1983–1988, which was much less than the 4.19% growth rate registered during 1978–1983.

Table 27 Average Annual Growth rate of GDP by Main
Sectors measured in 1981 constant factor cost (1974–1988)

Economic Sectors		1974–1978	1978–1983	1983–1988	1974–1988
Agriculture		-0.07	2.62	-3.24	-0.27
Industry		-1.73	6.99	3.82	3.31
Services		2	5.33	2.78	3.46

Total GDP 0.36 4.19 0.21 1.65
Source: ONCCP, based on Plan Document

While the TYPP was in process, major employment studies continued in the 1980s. The statistical and theoretical study[53] on industrialization assessed the significance of medium and large-scale enterprises and the necessity of their linkages to small-scale and handicraft industries, to the agricultural sector and to the raw material base of the country with a view to creating employment opportunities and increasing productivity.

The study on manufacturing enterprises in the 1970s and the early 1980s proved that the manufacturing sector was capital intensive. Table 28 (below) displays fixed capital assets, labor cost, employment, capital/labor, and labor/capital ratios in the Ethiopian manufacturing sector for the years, 1976/77-1982/83.

---

[53] Eshetu Chole and Teshome Mulat. *Patterns of Industrialization and Impact on Employment and Incomes in African Countries: The Case of Ethiopia*. (JASPA), Addis Ababa, 1983

Table 28 Fixed Capital Assets, Labor Cost and
Employment in Manufacturing Sector in Ethiopia

Yr	PK/PL	% Change	Fixed Cap Asset (in,000)	L/K	% Change	Labor Cost (in,000)	Number of Employees
1976/77	3.05		370.8	0.00017		121,491	62,807
1977/78	2.7	-11.4	354.8	0.00019	10	130,968	65,858
1978/79	2.3	114.8	351.2	0.00022	17.7	155,986	76,837
1979/80	2.2	-4.3	373.6	0.00021	-5.9	171,156	76,895
1981/82	2.2	0	427.3	0.00019	-6.7	193,240	82,165
1982/83	2.1	-4.5	450.4	0.00019	-3.12	211,811	83,732
Average Change	-7%				2,4%		

Source: CSO Survey of Manufacturing Industries, Addis Ababa (Jan 1980, May 1980, June 1981, April 1982, June 1984, Feb 1986

Note: PK/PL=Price of Capital and Price of Labor, L/K = Labor Capital Ratio.). As given in Table 28 (above), PK/PL is negative (-7%), and L/K is positive (+2.4%). The elasticity of substitution, (L/K)/(PK/PL) = (2.4)/ (-7) = -0.34 (author's computation). Therefore, the elasticity of substitution (-0.34) for the indicated years suggests that there was no room for factor price modification, which resulted in dim employment opportunity.

Notable employment studies of the decade were: a) Manpower Study,[54] which focused on tackling unemployment problem; b) School Leavers' Survey (1985), which was designed

---

[54] Manpower Implications of Current Development Strategies (vol. 1), Addis Ababa, Nov. 1984.

to track the number of unemployed school leavers and identify their needs; and c) Manpower Surveying and Planning (1987), which was initiated to create a better manpower planning machinery. Despite these efforts, the unemployment situation did not improve.

In general, the 1980s ended with an average GDP growth rate of 1.4%, which was incompatible with the labor force growth rate of 2.9%.[55] The bottom line is that the planned employment target (758,000) remained far from being achieved. The tariff structure was also a barrier to employment creation in Ethiopia. For details, see Appendix 3 (p. 185).

4. The Development Strategies of the 1990s to 2020

The Federal Democratic Republic of Ethiopia (FDRE) embarked on a series of development plans. The initial plan, Sustainable Development and Poverty Reduction Program (SDPRP),[56] took place during the years, 1992/1993–1999/2000. The overall goal of the plan was to reduce poverty head count ratio by 10% at the end of the program (2004/2005) from the poverty rate of 44% estimated during 1999/2000 based on the assumption that GDP would increase by 7% during the period of the program.

Fiscal and monetary policies, financial sector improvements, and equitable growth policies were considered as major strategies for achieving the poverty reduction goal. The growth policies focused on four key areas: a) Agricultural Development Led Industrialization (ADLI), b)

---

[55] World Development Report, 1990.

[56] SDPRP Report, MOFED, July 2004.

Justice System and Civil Service Reform, c) Decentralization and Empowerment, and d) Capacity Building in Public and Private sectors. At the end of the plan period (2004/2005), GDP increased by 5.9%, short of the expected target of 7%. However, poverty head count ratio decreased from the 1999 level of 44.2% to 38.7% in 2004.[57]

The government continued rolling out plans. In the second phase, the Plan for Accelerated and Sustainable Development to End Poverty (PASDEP) took place during the period, 2005/2006-2009/2010. The objective of the plan was to set "the directions for accelerated, sustained, and people-centered economic development as well as to pave the groundwork for the attainment of the Millennium Development Goals (MDGs) by 2015."[58] The results of the plan showed successful implementation (displayed in Table 29). Growth targets were achieved. Average GDP growth rate of 11% exceeded the base GDP growth rate of 7% estimated at the beginning of the plan period. The service sector of the economy registered the highest growth (14.6%).

[57] Based on World Bank data.

[58] Ethiopia: Building on Progress: A Plan for Accelerated and Sustained Development to End Poverty (PASDEP) (2005/06-2009/10) Volume I: Ministry of Finance and Economic Development (MoFED), 44.

Table 29 Growth targets and performance under PASDEP (2005/06–2009/10)

	Base Case (%)	High Case (%)	Average. Growth Achieved (%)
GDP (%)	7%	10%	11%
Agriculture and allied industries	6	6.4	8
Industry	11	18	10
Services	7	10.3	14.6

Source: Ministry of Finance and Economic Development (MOFED) Sep. 2010, 4.

Following the PASDEP, the Growth Transformation Plan (GTP) took place during the periods, 2010/2011 to 2014/2015. At the end of these two plan-periods (PASDEP and GTP), GDP increased by 11% and 10%, respectively. "Ethiopia's growth rate also exceeded regional and low-income averages over the past decade."[59]

---

[59] Ethiopia's Great Run, The Growth Acceleration and How to Pace It. World Bank, Feb. 2016, p.3

Poverty and Economic Growth in Ethiopia (1995/96–2015/16), Planning and Development Commission, (Addis Ababa, Dec 2018), 41.

Chart 12 GDP growth rates (1992/93-2014/15)

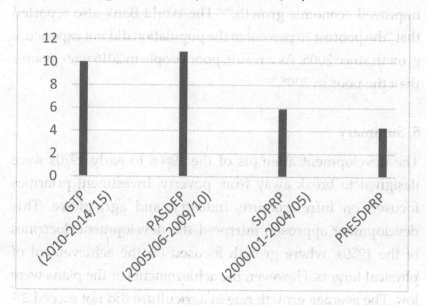

Chart created by author based on data for the plan periods.

Table 30 Poverty headcount ratio at the national poverty lines (% of Population) – Ethiopia

Year	Poverty head count ratio
1999	44.2
2004	38.7
2010	29.6
2015	23.5

Source: World Bank data.

Poverty headcount ratio decreased from the 2010 level of 29.6% to 23.5% in 2015. However, the overall poverty reduction has not reached the poorest members of the society. "Poverty severity index has increased in both urban and rural areas, indicating that the poorest of the poor are not benefitting from improved economic growth."[60] The World Bank also reported that "the poorest 10 percent of the population did not experience growth since 2005. As a result, poor people in 2016 were poorer than the poor in 2005."[61]

5. Summary

The development attempts of the 1960s to early 1970s were designed to break away from poverty. Investment priorities focused on infrastructure, industry, and agriculture. This development approach mirrored the development doctrines of the 1950s, where growth focused on the achievement of physical targets. However, the achievements of the plans were low. The average growth rate in agriculture did not exceed 2% per year, which was less than the population growth rate of 2.3%. The 1970s also witnessed unrest and regime change in Ethiopia. However, the development plan continued with the establishment of the Office of National Committee for Central Planning (ONCCP) in 1979.

The 1980s development strategy focused on three major objectives: a) ensuring the availability of sufficient supply of goods and services, b) increasing foreign exchange earnings, and c) starting the eradication of deep-seated social problems such as unemployment and illiteracy. Then the Ten-Year

---

[60] Poverty and Economic Growth in Ethiopia (1995/96–2015/16), Planning and Development Commission, (Addis Ababa, Dec 2018), 41.

[61] Poverty Assessment: Poverty Rate Declines Despite Challenges. World Bank, April 2020. https://www.worldbank.org/en/country/ethiopia/publication/ethiopia-poverty-assessment-poverty-rate.

Perspective Plan (TYPP) (1983/84–1993/94) was rolled out with the objective of achieving overall GDP growth rate of 6.5%. However, the implementation of the Five-Year Plan (of the TYPP) demonstrated shortfalls. Agriculture suffered a series of droughts, reaching the apex in 1985. The 1980s ended with an average GDP growth rate of 1.4%, which was incompatible with the labor force growth rate of 2.9%. The planned employment target of 758,000 also remained far from being achieved.

Development plans continued in the 1990s. The Sustainable Development and Poverty Reduction Program (SDPRP) took place during 1992/1993–1999/2000. At the end of the program (2004/2005), GDP growth rate increased by 5.9%, short of the expected target of 7%. However, poverty head count ratio decreased from the 1999 level of 44.2% to 38.7% in 2004. Then, the Ethiopian government rolled out the Plan for Accelerated and Sustainable Development to End Poverty (PASDEP) during 2005/2006–2009/2010. The result of the plan showed successful implementation. Growth targets were achieved. Average GDP Growth rate of 11% exceeded the base GDP growth rate of 7%.

Following the PASDEP, the First Growth Transformation Plan (GTPI) took place between 2010/2011 and 2014/2015. At the end of the plan period, GDP increased by 10%. The economic growth of Ethiopia also surpassed regional and low-income averages over the past decade. Poverty head count decreased from the 2010 level of 29.6% to 23.5% in 2015. However, the poorest 10% of the population did not experience growth since 2005. As a result, poor people in 2016 were poorer than the poor in 2005.

The Second Growth Transformation Plan (GTPII) 2015/16–2019/20 was then rolled out. The objective of the plan is to elevate Ethiopia's economy to a lower-middle income country. Having met six of the eight Millennium Development Goals (MDGs), Ethiopia is bent on accelerating the implementation of the 2030 Sustainable Development Goals. The eight MDGs include the following: 1) eradicate extreme poverty and hunger, 2) achieve universal primary education, 3) promote gender equality and empower women, 4) reduce child mortality, 5) improve maternal health, 6) combat HIV/AIDS, malaria, and other diseases, 7) ensure environmental sustainability, and 8) employ global partnership for development. Out of the above eight goals, the two goals, "gender equality and women empowerment" and "improvement of maternal health," were not met.

CHAPTER IV

The Impact of the Environment on the Poor

1. Introduction

In nature, everything is connected. To sustain life, we need to take care of the environment, and foster inclusive development programs. This chapter addresses the impact of environmental factors on the poor. The health hazards of air pollution, deforestation, greenhouse gas emissions, and unsafe water will be discussed with the help of data. The connection between environment and growth, and the impact of land tenure and productivity will be addressed. The chapter also highlights the Ethiopian Government's attempts in terms of tackling pollution and poverty.

2. Overview

> In nature, everything is connected. This is equally true of a healthy environment and a healthy economy. We cannot hope to sustain life without taking care of nature. And we need

healthy economies to lift people out of poverty and achieve the United Nations Sustainable Development Goals. In our current model these goals sometimes seem to collide, and our economic pursuits encroach too closely on nature. But nature—a stable climate, reliable freshwater, forests, and other natural resources— is what makes industry possible. It is not one or the other. We cannot have long-term human development without a steady climate and a healthy natural world[62].

The above remark underlines the symbiotic relationship between a healthy environment and a healthy economy. However, compelling evidence reflects that economic growth is taking place at the expense of the environment. The "world's richest 1% cause double CO_2 emissions of poorest 50%, says Oxfam."[63]

The fact of the matter is that rich countries have outsourced pollution (carbon footprint) to China and emerging economies. *The New York Times* reported that "wealthy countries have effectively 'outsourced' a big chunk of their carbon pollution overseas, by importing more steel, cement, and other goods

---

[62] The Economics of Climate, IMF F &D, Dec. 2019. P.5. Retrieved from: https://www.imf.org/external/pubs/ft/andd/2019/12/pdf/fd1219.pdf

[63] Fiona Harvey, The Guardian, 20 Sept 2020 https://www.the guardian.com/environment/2020/sep/21/worlds-richest-1-cause-double-c02-emission

from factories in China and other places, rather than producing it domestically."[64]

The IMF Finance and Development Report underlines the climate change risks in terms of physical, transitional, and other potential risks. The physical risks are triggered by extreme weather conditions and gradual changes in climate, causing damage to land, infrastructure, and property. The transitional risks emanate from changes in climate policy, technology, and consumer preferences during the process of "adjustment to a lower-carbon economy."[65]

3. Air Pollution, Deforestation and Access to Electricity

3.1 Air Pollution

Most recorded air pollution–linked deaths occur in developing countries, where laws are weak or not applied, vehicle emission standards are less stringent and coal power stations more prevalent. And in the big cities of developing countries, it's the poorest who live in cramped informal settlements, often near rubbish dumps, who feel the full force of air pollution.[66]

In a *Lancet* report, the visibility study conducted between 1974

---

[64] Brad Plumer, The New York Times, Sept 4, 2018You've Heard of Outsourced Jobs, but Outsourced Pollution? It's real, and Tough to Tally Up https://www.nytimes.com/2018/09/04/climate/outsourcing-carbon-emissions.html

[65] The Economics of Climate, IMF F&D, Dec. 2019, p.26 https://www.imf.org/external/pubs/ft/fandd/2019/12/pdf/fd1219.pdf

[66] UN Environment Programme, Air pollution hurts the poorest most, 09 May 2019. Retrieved from: https://www.unenvironment.org/news-and-stories/story/air-pollution-hurts-poorest-most.

and 2018 in Addis Ababa, Nairobi, and Kampala demonstrated a significant decrease in visibility. "Air pollution increased by 62% in Addis Ababa, 162% in Kampala, and 182% in Nairobi."[67] "Data on air quality are crucial to guide policy making and to address the challenges caused by poor air quality among various stakeholders," says Gabriel Okello, director of African Centre of Clean Air, based in Kampala, Uganda, according to the above *Lancet* Report on Air Pollution in Africa.

3.2 Deforestation

Deforestation has a devastating impact on the environment. "Natural resources are being depleted, clean air is growing scarce, climates are shifting, and entire ecosystems are being affected. It doesn't take long to look around the world and see the ways in which the environment is changing. While mankind, in general, places stress on the environment, poverty has played a major role in environmental degradation."[68] Land depletion due to erosion, and dry weather contribute to pollution. "Agricultural livestock are responsible for a large proportion of global greenhouse gas emissions, most notably methane. In addition, overgrazing is a major problem regarding environmental sustainability."[69]

---

[67] Air Pollution in Africa, Munyardzi Makoni, *The Lancet*, July 2020. Retrieved from: https://www.thelancet.com/journals/lanres/article/PIIS2213-2600(20)30275-7/fulltext.

[68] The Borgen Project, Oct 2, 2013 How Poverty Impacts the Environment | The Borgen Project.

[69] National Geographic Article, May 11, 2020. Accessed December 3, 2020. Retrieved from: Environmental Impacts of Agricultural Modifications | National Geographic Society.

According to FAO, "forests provide more than 86 million green jobs and support the livelihoods of many more …. Of the people living in extreme poverty, over 90 percent are dependent on forests for at least part of their livelihoods."[70] Forests also help to clean the environment by taking in carbon dioxide and by providing habitable place for "eighty percent of the world's land species."[71] However, it takes investment and time to preserve forests as society transitions from the daily use of firewood for cooking and heating to the use of electric oven or range.

3.3 Access to Electricity

According to the World Development Report, about 90% of the world's population has access to electricity. However, the picture is different regarding sub-Saharan Africa: only 48% of the population has access to electricity. In Ethiopia, electricity is accessible to 45% of the population. Therefore, most households (55%) resort to the daily use of wood, charcoal, or dung for cooking and heating. This continued practice compounds the problem of pollution, contributing to health hazards.

Table 31 Access to Electricity (% of population) 2018

World	89.57
North America	100

[70] FAO, The State of the World's Forests, 2020 http://www.fao.org/state-of-forests/en

[71] World WildLife (WWF), Deforestation and Forest Degradation. https://www.worldwildlife.org/threats/deforestation-and-forest-degradation.

European Union	100
Sub-Saharan Africa	47.7
(Ethiopia)	45
Latin America & Caribbean	98.3
Middle East & North Africa	95.9

Source: World Bank
https://data.worldbank.org/indicator/EG.ELC.ACCS.ZS

4. CO2 and Greenhouse Gas Emissions

The data[72] on CO_2 emissions per capita (for 2017) shows that high income countries emit more pollutants. However, in high income countries, the share of population living in extreme poverty is 0.70%. For the world, CO_2 emissions per capita (for 2017) was estimated at 4.79 tons, and the global share of population living in extreme poverty was 10% in 2015, and for sub-Saharan Africa, it was 41%. For Ethiopia, CO_2 emissions per capita is 0.14 tons, and the share of population living in extreme poverty is 26.7%. Chart 13 displays the trend in CO_2 emissions from 1948 to 2017.

[72] Source: Our World in Data. Retrieved from: https://ourworldindata.org/grapher/co-emissions-per-capita-vs-the-share-of-people-living-in-extreme-poverty.

Chart 13 Per Capita CO$_2$ Emissions

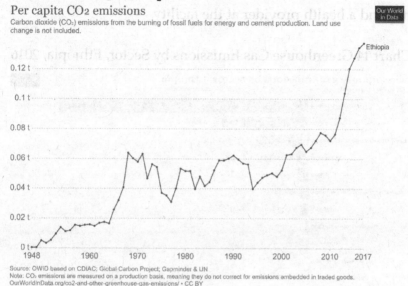

Per capita CO2 emissions

Carbon dioxide (CO₂) emissions from the burning of fossil fuels for energy and cement production. Land use change is not included.

Source: OWID based on CDIAC; Global Carbon Project; Gapminder & UN
Note: CO₂ emissions are measured on a production basis, meaning they do not correct for emissions embedded in traded goods.
OurWorldInData.org/co2-and-other-greenhouse-gas-emissions/ • CC BY

(Note: According to Encyclopedia Britannica, Carbon dioxide (CO$_2$) is "a colorless gas that has a faint, sharp odor, and a slightly sour taste.")

The sectoral breakdown of greenhouse gas emissions (Chart 14) shows that agriculture accounts for 57% of total emissions. This has a huge impact on the health of the rural population of Ethiopia, where access to healthcare is sparsely distributed. This situation is even more severe for women. In a report released by demographic and health survey, 98%[73] of women expressed lack of money, long distance to healthcare, and inaccessible roads, or roads in poor condition as causing their difficulty of access to

---

[73] Central Statistical Agency [Ethiopia] and ICF International. 2012. Ethiopia Demographic and Health Survey 2011. Addis Ababa, Ethiopia and Calverton, Maryland, USA: Central Statistical Agency and ICF International. Ethiopia Demographic and Health Survey 2011 (dhsprogram.com).

healthcare. Women also stated their concerns that they would not find a health provider at the facility.

Chart 14 Greenhouse Gas Emissions by Sector, Ethiopia, 2016

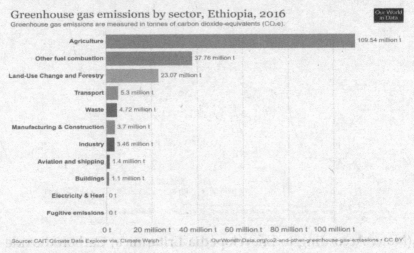

Greenhouse gas emissions by sector, Ethiopia, 2016
Greenhouse gas emissions are measured in tonnes of carbon dioxide-equivalents (CO₂e).

Sector	Emissions
Agriculture	109.54 million t
Other fuel combustion	37.76 million t
Land-Use Change and Forestry	23.07 million t
Transport	5.3 million t
Waste	4.72 million t
Manufacturing & Construction	3.7 million t
Industry	3.46 million t
Aviation and shipping	1.4 million t
Buildings	1.1 million t
Electricity & Heat	0 t
Fugitive emissions	0 t

0 t   20 million t   40 million t   60 million t   80 million t   100 million t

Source: CAIT Climate Data Explorer via. Climate Watch   OurWorldInData.org/co2-and-other-greenhouse-gas-emissions • CC BY

Source: Our World in Data

Note: According to Encyclopedia Britannica, "greenhouse is any gas that has the property of absorbing infrared radiation (net heat energy) emitted from Earth's surface and reradiating it back to earth's surface, thus contributing to the greenhouse effect. Carbon dioxide, methane, and water vapor are the most important greenhouse gases" (greenhouse gas | Definition, Emissions, & Greenhouse Effect | Britannica).

5. Unsafe Water

Lack of safe water, inadequate sanitation and hygiene are also pressing environmental issues that lay heavy burdens on the poor. In the case of Ethiopia, "60–80 percent of communicable diseases, and 50 percent of the consequence of undernutrition is attributed to limited access to safe water and inadequate sanitation and hygiene services."[74]

The following chart displays the share of deaths from unsafe water (from 1990 to 2017) for Ethiopia, Chad, sub-Saharan Africa, and the world.

As you see from the chart, in the case of Ethiopia, the share of death from unsafe water increased from 7.14% in 1990 to 8.9% in 2017. In the extreme case, Chad has experienced more deaths (14.45%) for 2017. For sub-Saharan Africa countries, the share of deaths from unsafe water declined from 9.21% to 6.05%, and for the world, the death rate declined from 4.54% to 2.2% between 1990 and 2017.

Chart 15

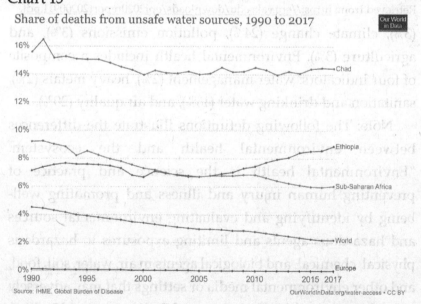

Share of deaths from unsafe water sources, 1990 to 2017

Source: IHME, Global Burden of Disease

OurWorldInData.org/water-access · CC BY

Source: Our World in Data, https://ourworldindata.org/water-access.

---

[74] UNICEF Ethiopia, 2018. Water, sanitation, and hygiene (WASH) | UNICEF Ethiopia.

6. Environmental Performance Index (EPI)**

The EPI framework organizes 32 indicators into 11 issue categories and two policy objectives, with weights shown at each level as a percentage of the total score. The 11 issues include air quality (20%), biodiversity & habitat (15%), ecosystem services (6%), fisheries (6%), water resources (3%), climate change (24%), pollution emissions (3%), waste management (2%), heavy metals (2%), agriculture (3%), and sanitation and drinking water (16%).

The two policy issues focus on ecosystem vitality (60%) and environmental health (40%). Ecosystem vitality includes a composite of seven indicators: biodiversity and habitat (15%), ecosystem services (6%), fisheries (6%), water resources

** EPI, Yale Center for Environment Law & Policy, Yale University. Retrieved from: https://epi.yale.edu/downloads/epi2020report20200911.pdf.

(3%), climate change (24%), pollution emissions (3%), and agriculture (3%). Environmental health includes a composite of four indicators: water management (2%), heavy metals (2%), sanitation and drinking water (16%), and air quality (20%).

Note: The following definitions illustrate the differences between environmental health and the ecosystem. "Environmental health is the science and practice of preventing human injury and illness and promoting well-being by identifying and evaluating environmental sources and hazardous agents and limiting exposures to hazardous physical, chemical, and biological agents in air, water, soil, food, and other environmental media or settings that may adversely affect human health" (Definitions of Environmental Health | National Environmental Health Association: NEHA).

"An ecosystem is a geographic area where plants, animals, and other organisms, as well as weather and landscape work together to form a bubble of life. Ecosystems contain biotic or living parts, as well as abiotic factors, or nonliving parts. Biotic factors include plants, animals, and other organisms. Abiotic factors include rocks, temperature, and humidity" (Ecosystem | National Geographic Society).

Table 32 (below) shows the environmental performance ranking index (EPI) for the top ten and the bottom ten countries. Denmark ranks first, followed by Luxembourg (second), Switzerland (third), United Kingdom (fourth), France (fifth), Austria (sixth), Finland (seventh), Sweden (eighth), Norway (ninth), and Germany (tenth). Ethiopia ranks 134th out of 180 countries. The bottom ten countries in the list include: Haiti, Chad, Solomon Islands, Madagascar, Guinea, Côte d'Ivoire, Sierra Leone, Afghanistan, Myanmar, and Liberia.

Table 32 Environmental Performance Index (EPI) (2020)
Top Ten Countries

	Score	Rank
Denmark	82.5	1
Luxembourg	82.3	2
Switzerland	81.5	3
United Kingdom	81.3	4
France	80	5
Austria	79.6	6
Finland	78.9	7
Sweden	78.7	8
Norway	77.7	9
Germany	77.2	10
Ethiopia	34.4	134

Table 32 EPI (2020)
Bottom Ten Countries

Haiti	27	171
Chad	26.7	172
Solomon Islands	26.7	172
Madagascar	26.5	174
Guinea	26.4	175
Cote d'Ivoire	25.8	176
Sierra Leone	25.7	177
Afghanistan	25.5	178
Myanmar	25.1	179
Liberia	22.6	180

Source: EPI, Yale Center for Environment Law & Policy, Yale University
https://epi.yale.edu/downloads/epi2020report20200911.pdf

7. Environment and Economic Growth

The advocates of growth argue that growth, accompanied by technological advances, does help countries to use "fewer natural resources and mitigate their environmental impact."[75] However, available evidence shows a different picture. The International Resource Panel Report states that material resource use is expected to more than double from 2015 to 2050,[76] prompting urgency for a better and efficient utilization

---

[75] Matei Alexianu, Is green growth possible? Revisiting the Environmental Kuznets curve. Industrial Growth Center (IGC), January 2, 2019. Retrieved from: Is green growth possible? Revisiting the Environmental Kuznets curve - IGC (theigc.org).

[76] U.N. Environment, Dec. 2017. Retrieved from: https://www.unenvironment.org/news-and-stories/press-release/resource-use-expected-double-2050-better-natural-resource-use.

of natural resources. On the other hand, "degrowth" advocates push for reduced production. "Degrowth does not mean decay or suffering …. Instead, degrowth can be compared to a healthy diet voluntarily undertaken. The material footprint (or resource use) of combined OECD nations increased by almost 50% between 1990 and 2008—every 10% rise in GDP saw a 6% increase in material footprint. But that is where a theory called 'degrowth' could come in: it argues that sharply reducing working hours and consumption will save the world."[77]

7.1 The Environmental Kuznets Curve (EKC)

EKC posits an inverted U relationship between growth and pollution. It means that during the initial phase of development, as the economy grows, pollution increases. However, with increased growth, and increased income, "leading industrial sectors become cleaner, people value the environment more highly, and regulatory institutions become more effective." As a result, "pollution levels off in the middle-income range and then falls towards pre-industrial levels in wealthy societies."[78]

Dasgupta et al. (2002) explored different perspectives about the application of EKC. The research focused on the proponents of the model (including applied econometricians), the pessimists, and the pragmatists. However, Dasgupta et al. argue that developing countries could lower and flatten

---

[77] Tim Smedley, *BBC Worklife*, 22 July 2019. Retrieved from: https://www.bbc.com/worklife/article/20190718-degrowth

[78] Susmita Dasgupta, Benoit Laplante, Hua Wang, David Wheeler, "Confronting the Environmental Kuznets Curve" in *Journal of Economic Perspectives*, 08953309, Winter 2002, Vol. 16, Issue 1, 147.

the EKC "by financing appropriate training, policy reforms, information gathering, and public environmental education."[79]

Bottom Line: EKC has triggered discussion and debate about its application. In the debate, the role of social media is gaining momentum in terms of creating awareness about the impact of pollution. Environmental advocates are also putting pressure on businesses to invest in green economy.

8. Land Tenure

Land property rights provide incentives for farmers to invest in the land and generate higher yields. In other words, land rights help farmers earn more income. Owning land certificate also helps farmers to access credit using the certificate as a collateral. The other benefit of title ownership is that it "reduces the time and resources spent by households to defend their claims of land, which frees up resources that can be invested in human capital of households 'or in income-generating activities."[80] However, when property rights do not exist, and when farmers feel they can be evicted from farming on short notice, the tendency to invest in the land decreases. As a result, productivity diminishes, and farmers' income also decreases.

Steven Lawry and his team reviewed many studies and identified 100 studies on the topic and selected 20 studies to understand the impact of land tenure on farm productivity in five countries in Asia, in five countries in Latin America, and

---

[79] Dasgupta et al, "Confronting the Environmental Kuznets Curve," 164.

[80] Felix M. Muchomba, "Women's Land Tenure Security and Household Human Capital: Evidence from Ethiopia's Land Certification," in *World Development*, vol. 98, 310–324; p 311 http://dx.doi.org/10.1016/j.worlddev.2017.04.034.

in ten countries in Africa. Ethiopia was included in the study. The findings show evidence about the strong link between land ownership (with titles or certificates) and productivity growth of "between 50 to 100 percent" in Asia and Latin America. However, in the case of Africa, productivity showed "relatively modest gains."[81] One major reason explaining the slow productivity gains in Africa is the low level of investment in the farming sector.

Felix M. Muchomba[82] also researched women's land tenure security and household human capital to assess the impact of land title on women's decision power based on data from the Ethiopian Rural Household Survey (ERHS), a longitudinal survey of 147 households from the four major regions in Ethiopia (Tigray, Amhara, Oromia, and SNNP). His conclusion reflects that the inclusion of women in land certification increased their decision-making power in terms of household production and spending.

9. The Global Response and Ethiopia's Effort to Combating Pollution

A global response to slow CO_2 and greenhouse emissions is set in the 2015 Paris Agreement. Advanced economies voluntarily agreed (pledged) to reduce emissions by 20 to 40 percent by 2030.[83] On top of that, a tax increase on carbon has also been

---

[81] *Forests News*, Steven Lawry, Tuesday, 24 February 2015, "How does land tenure affect agricultural productivity? A systematic review," https://forestsnews.cifor.org/26908/land-tenure-reforms-africa-review?fnl

[82] Muchomba, "Women's Land Tenure Security", 321.

[83] *The Economics of Climate*, IMF F&D, December 2019, 16. https://www.imf.org/external/pubs/ft/fandd/2019/12/pdf/fd1219.pdf

proposed as an incentive for pursuing investment in clean energy technology. And member nations, including Ethiopia, are tasked with the responsibility of curbing pollution using better technology and improved methods of production.

Environmental pollution affects the poor across the board. Urban congestion and lack of sanitation and waste disposal aggravate the problem in the absence of investment in urban infrastructure. Therefore, it is critical to strengthen cities' resources to manage these difficulties as Ethiopia's urban population keeps on rising.

To combat poverty and lift Ethiopia to the status of a middle-income country by 2025, a Climate-Resilient Green Economy (CRGE) strategy is set in motion to "bypass the conventional approach to economic development and create a green economy, where economic development goals are met in a sustainable way."[84] To this end, the strategy identifies the four development pillars in the green economic action plan to "a) improve crop and livestock production practices for higher food security and farmer income while reducing emissions, b) protect and re-establish forests for their economic and ecosystem services, including as carbon stocks, c) expand electricity generation from renewable sources of energy for domestic and regional markets, and d) leapfrog to modern and energy-efficient technologies in transport, industrial sectors, and buildings."[85]

---

[84] *Ethiopia's Climate-Resilient Green Economy*, (CRGE), Federal Democratic Republic of Ethiopia, 2011.Sustainable Development Goals. Accessed Dec. 4, 2020 https://sustainabledevelopment

[85] CRGE.

10. Summary

Pollution is a global concern. Major polluters are the world's richest 1 percent. Most air pollution–linked deaths occur in developing countries where laws are weak and not applied. About 90% of the world's population has access to electricity. However, access to electricity is only available to 48% of the population in sub-Saharan Africa (on average) and to 45% of the population in Ethiopia. Therefore, most households in sub-Saharan Africa, including Ethiopia, resort to the daily use of firewood, charcoal, or dung for cooking and heating purposes.

The Grand Ethiopian Renaissance Dam, expected to be completed by 2030, will not only fulfill Ethiopia's chronic electricity shortage, but it will also position the country in a trajectory to be the largest electric exporter in Africa. Additional benefits of the dam include flood mitigation and enhanced irrigation of new agricultural land. Overall, the dam will contribute to economic growth and employment opportunities.

The data on CO_2 emissions per capita show that high-income countries emit more pollutants. However, in high-income countries, the share of population living in extreme poverty is 0.70%. For the world, CO_2 emissions per capita were estimated at 4.79 tons (for 2017). The global share of population living in extreme poverty was 10% in 2015, and for sub-Saharan Africa, it was 41%. For Ethiopia, CO_2 emissions per capita were estimated at 0.14 tons, and the share of population living in extreme poverty was estimated at 26.7%.

In Ethiopia, unsafe water causes 60 to 80% of communicable diseases and 50% of the consequence of undernutrition. Unsafe water also contributes to deaths. For Ethiopia, the share of deaths from unsafe water increased from 7.14% in 1990 to 8.9%

in 2017. This chapter also mentioned the importance of land property rights as an incentive for farmers to invest in farming, and to generate higher yields and income.

To combat the adverse effects of climate change, advanced economies voluntarily agreed (pledged) to reduce emissions by 20 to 40 percent by 2030. On top of that, a tax increase on carbon has also been proposed as an incentive for pursuing investment in clean energy technology. The Ethiopian government is also moving in a direction to reduce poverty and lift the country to the status of a middle-income economy by 2025, using a Climate-Resilient Green Economy (CRGE) development strategy.

CHAPTER V

The Impact of Corruption and COVID-19 on Economic Growth and the Poor

1. Introduction

This chapter explores the impact of corruption on economic growth and the poor. Data on Corruption Perception Index (CPI) and Trace Bribery Risk Matrix will be used to identify country rankings and voice concerns. Evidence shows that pervasive corruption takes place in Ethiopia. The chapter also addresses the impact of the COVID-19 pandemic on economic growth and the poor. Then the discussion highlights the participation of the international organizations with the Ethiopian government in terms of tackling the pandemic.

2. Overview

The World Bank defines corruption as the abuse of public office for private gain. Corruption manifests in different forms: bribery, theft, fraud, and political corruption. "Corruption has a disproportionate impact on the poor and most vulnerable, increasing costs and reducing access to services, including health, education, and justice. Corruption in the procurement of drugs and medical equipment drives up costs and can lead to sub-standard or harmful products. The human costs of counterfeit drugs and vaccinations on health outcomes and the life-long impacts on children far exceed the financial costs. Unofficial payments for services can have a particularly pernicious effect on poor people."[86]

How is corruption measured?

According to Transparency International, corruption is measured based on the Corruption Perception Index (CPI). "The CPI scores and ranks countries/territories based on how corrupt a country's public sector is perceived to be by experts and business executives. It is a composite index, a combination of 13 surveys, and assessments of corruption, collected by a variety of reputable institutions. The CPI is the most widely used indicator of corruption worldwide."[87]

Based on data from the World Economic Forum,[88] Denmark, New Zealand, Finland, Singapore, Sweden, Switzerland, and Norway are the least corrupt countries. Somalia, Syria, South Sudan, Yemen, and North Korea are most corrupt countries. Table 33 (below) includes the CPI of least and most corrupt countries.

---

[86] Combating Corruption, World Bank https://www.worldbank.org/en/topic/governance/brief/anti-corruption.

[87] Transparency International https://www.transparency.org/en/cpi/2020/index/nzl#.

[88] World Economic Forum, Feb 3, 2020. Retrieved from: https://www.weforum.org/agenda/2020/02/global-corruption-transparency-international-index/.

Table 33 Corruption Perception Index (CPI) 2020

Least Corrupt Countries	Corruption Perception Index
Denmark	88/100
New Zealand	87/100
Finland	85/100
Singapore	85/100
Sweden	85/100
Switzerland	85/100
Norway	84/100

Most Corrupt Countries	Corruption Perception Index
Venezuela	15/100
Yemen	15/100
Syria	14/100
Somalia	12/100
South Sudan	12/100

Source: Transparency International. https://www.transparency.org/en/cpi/2020/index/nzl

According to Transparency International, the average Corruption Perception Index (CPI) for sub-Saharan Africa is 32; for East Europe and Central Asia, it is 35; and for Ethiopia, it is 38. Table 34 shows Ethiopia's global ranking regarding corruption.

Table 34 Ethiopia's global ranking in corruption

Year	Ranking
2010	116
2011	120
2012	113
2013	111

2014	110
2015	103
2016	108
2017	107
2018	114
2019	96

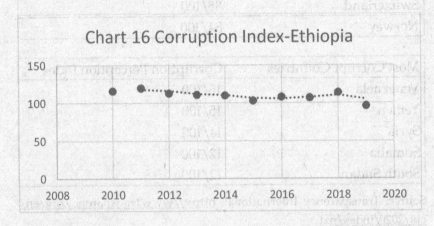

Chart 16 Corruption Index-Ethiopia

Source: Transparency International. https://www.transparency.org/en/countries/ethiopia

The issues regarding corruption have triggered debates. Some studies support corruption from the perspective of a "grease the wheel" approach, which underlines the need to pay bribes to avoid stringent and impassable bureaucratic regulation to operate a business and eke out a living. "There is a strand in the corruption literature, contributed both by economists and non-economists, corruption may [actually] improve efficiency and help growth."[89] Most research findings, however, highlight that corruption brings with it a host of negative factors. I will address the negative impacts of corruption in the following paragraphs.

3. The Impacts of Corruption on the Society and on Growth

3.1 Government Corruption

Society loses when corrupt governments take power and enrich themselves at the expense of the society. Money that should have been channeled for development is squandered with no accountability. Daron Acemoglu and James A. Robinson wrote a piece in the *Wall Street Journal* under the tittle "Corruption Is Just a Symptom, Not the Disease." They proposed that the solution is to create institutions that work for people instead of tolerating "existing structures that typically serve the narrow, graft-addicted elites that often suck poor nations dry."[90]

3.2 Corruption and Poverty

Corruption aggravates poverty. According to Transparency International, "corruption hits the poor the most" and "goes

---

[89] Pranab Bardhan, "Corruption and Development: A Review of Issues," in *Journal of Economic Literature*, Sep. 1997, Vol. 35, No. 3 (Sep. 1997), 1322. https://www.jstor.org/stable/2729979.

[90] Daron Acemoglu and James A. Robinson, "Corruption Is Just a Symptom, Not the Disease," *The Wall Street Journal*, Dec. 3, 2015. Retrieved from: https://www.wsj.com/articles/corruption-is-just-a-symptom-not-the-disease-1449174010.

beyond the bribe paid, the law violated, or the money stolen. It hits at the core of people's right to live better lives."[91]

Trace International, which compiles data on bribery, ranks countries based on their bribery risk scores, which are categorized in five parts, ranging from very low risk to very high risk. The very low risk category is represented by a score of 1 to 23; the low-risk range includes 23 to 41; the moderate risk range is represented by a score of 41 to 59; the high risk, by 59 to 78; the very high risk, by 78 to 100. Table 35 (below) includes country ranking and risk score.

Table 35 Bribery Risk Score by Country

Rank	Top 10 Countries	Risk Score
1	New Zealand	4
2	Norway	7
3	Denmark	7
4	Sweden	8
5	Finland	9
6	United Kingdom	11
7	Netherlands	12
8	Canada	14
9	Germany	15
10	Hong Kong	16

Trace Bribery Risk Matrix. www.traceinternational.org/trace-matrix

---

[91] "Ending Corruption to End Poverty," Transparency International, 25 September 2013. https://www.transparency.org/en/news/ending-corruption-to-end-poverty.

Rank	Bottom-Ten Countries	Risk score
200	Somalia	94
199	South Sudan	92
198	North Korea	86
197	Yemen	85
196	Venezuela	85
195	Chad	84
194	Libya	82
193	Turkmenistan	83
192	Equatorial Guinea	82
191	Dem. Rep of Congo	82
176	Ethiopia	71

Trace Bribery Risk Matrix. www.traceinternational.org/trace-matrix

Table 35 (above) includes the top ten countries with very low bribery risks, and the bottom ten countries with very high bribery risks, reported for 2019. From the list of the top ten countries, New Zealand ranks number 1, with a risk score of 4, followed by Norway, Denmark, Sweden, and Finland. Then the risk score increases to double digits, starting with the United Kingdom's risk score of 11 to Hong Kong's risk score of 16.

From the list of the bottom ten countries, Somalia stands out as the most corrupt country with a risk score of 94, followed by South Sudan, with a risk score of 92, and North Korea, with a risk score of 86. The other seven countries included in the list are Yemen, ranking 197, Venezuela, ranking 196, Chad, ranking 195, Libya, ranking 194, Turkmenistan, ranking 193, Equatorial Guinea, ranking 192, and Democratic Republic of

Congo, ranking 191 out of 200 countries. Ethiopia, which ranks 176th out of 200 countries, with a risk score of 71, is listed as a high-risk country for bribery.

Corruption and poverty are interrelated. Based on data from 97countries, including Ethiopia (between 1997 and 2000), "the empirical findings suggest that corruption and poverty go together, with causality running in both directions."[92] The evidence paper, "Why Corruption Matters"[93] also underlines that corruption "is likely to raise income inequality and affect the poor disproportionately."[94] The World Economic Forum warns that ending poverty should start with stopping corruption,[95] which disproportionately affects the poor.

3.3 *Corruption and Growth*

Corruption has adverse effects on growth and investment. "A one-standard-deviation improvement in the corruption index is estimated to be associated with an increase in the investment rate by about 3 percent of GDP."[96]

---

[92] Vahideh Negin, The Causal Relationship between Corruption and Poverty: A Panel Data Analysis, January 2010. Retrieved from: file:///C:/Users/Owner/Downloads/causality_between_corruption_and_poverty.pdf

[93] "Why Corruption Matters: understanding causes, effectiveness and how to address them," The UK Department for International Development, January 2015, 46.
https://www.gov.uk/government/organisations/department-for-international-development.

[94] IBID

[95] World Economic Forum, Jan 23, 2015 https://www.weforum.org/agenda/2015/01/want-to-end-poverty-start-with-corruption.

[96] Bardhan, "Corruption and Development," 1328.

From a theoretical perspective, corruption reduces economic growth in different ways. It acts as taxation and creates disincentive for investment. Corruption also breeds rent-seeking behavior by engaging people away from productive activities. Empirical analysis has "provided evidence of the negative effects of corruption on economic growth."[97]

Klaus Grundler and Niklas Potrafke provide analysis on corruption and economic growth based on empirical evidence. The authors' hypothesis: "grease the wheel" predicts corruption increases economic growth. However, empirical findings support the notion that corruption decreases economic growth. The authors used data "over the period, 2012–2018—a period for which the CPI is comparable across countries and over time— and concluded that "real per capita GDP decreased by around 17% in the long-run when the reversed Corruption Perception Index (CPI) increased by one standard deviation."[98] The authors also expressed the importance of reducing corruption: "When low corruption promotes economic growth—accelerated by good governance and transmitted by channels such as Foreign Direct investment (FDI)—citizens and policymakers have tools at hand to influence economic growth: fighting corruption,

---

[97] Raffaella Copier, Mauro Costantini, and Gustavo Piga, "The Role of Monitoring of Corruption in a Simple Endogenous Growth Model," in *Economic Inquiry*, Vol. 51, No. 4, October 2013, 1972.

[98] Klaus Grundler and Niklas Potrafke, "Corruption and economic growth: New empirical evidence," in *European Journal of Political Economy*, Vol. 60, Dec. 2019, Article 101810. Corruption and economic growth: New empirical evidence - ScienceDirect.

improving governance and democracy, and attracting foreign investors."[99]

4. COVID-19 and Its Impact on the Poor

4.1 Global Trend

The COVID-19 pandemic has triggered millions of deaths and contributed to the contraction of the global economy. The World Bank estimates a 5.2 percent decline in GDP, "the deep[est] recession in decades ... expected to leave lasting scars through lower investment, an erosion of human capital through lost work and schooling, and fragmentation of global trade and supply linkages."[100]

The United Nations estimates that the pandemic "will push 71 million people back into extreme poverty in 2020, in what would be the first rise in global poverty since 1998."[101]

---

[99] Gundler and Potrafke, 101810.

[100] "The Global Economic Outlook During the COVID-19 Pandemic: A Changing World," World Bank, June 18, 2020.

[101] "The Sustainable Development Goals Report," UN, 2020, 3.

Fig 1
Most countries are expected to face recessions in 2020

Share of economies in recession, 1871-2021

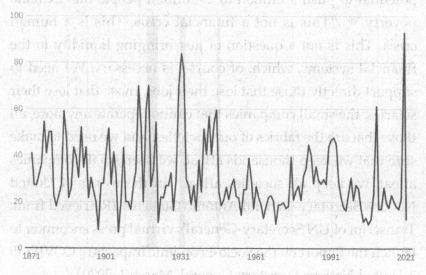

The proportion of economies with an annual contraction in per capita GDP. Shaded areas refer to global recessions. Data for 2020-21 are forecasts.
Source: World Bank

Source: World Bank

The World Food Program, which has consistently delivered food assistance to poor people all over the world since 1962, asserts that the COVID-19 pandemic would push an additional 300 million people into starvation.[102]

4.2 *The Trend in Africa*

The UN Economic Commission for Africa also portrays the impact of the pandemic on the lives of poor Africans who live in overcrowded slum areas and on Africa's economy. "Growth

---

[102] CNN. Retrieved from: https://www.cnn.com/2020/10/09/europe/world-food-programme-nobel.

could be slowing to 1.8 per cent in the best-case scenario or a contraction of 2.6 per cent in the worst case. This has the potential to push 5 million to 29 million people into extreme poverty."[103] "This is not a financial crisis. This is a human crisis. This is not a question of just bringing liquidity to the financial systems, which, of course, is necessary. We need to support directly those that lose their jobs, those that lose their salaries, the small companies that cannot operate anymore, all those that are the fabrics of our societies, and we need to make sure that we keep thousands afloat, we keep small companies afloat, we keep all societies afloat," in the words of United Nations Secretary-General António Guterres. (Retrieved from: Transcript of UN Secretary-General's virtual press encounter to launch the Report on the Socio-Economic Impacts of COVID-19 | United Nations Secretary-General, March 1, 2020.)

Sub-Saharan Africa countries are also experiencing weak health infrastructure, with low ratios of hospital beds, and health professionals per 1000 people. For medicine and pharmaceuticals, sub-Saharan Africa is also dependent on imports. "The price of life-saving medicine in Africa, where the need is greatest and the poverty is worst, is often higher than in Europe and North America, according to a study issued here today."[104]To combat the crisis, the report identifies mobilizing finance in the amount of $100 billion" [105] with emphasis on

---

[103] "COVID-19 in Africa," Economic Commission in Africa, Addis Ababa, April 2020, 8–9. Retrieved from: https://www.uneca.org/publications/covid-19-africa-protecting-lives-and-economies4.

[104] *New York Times*, June 17, 2000. https://www.nytimes.com/.

[105] See Economic Commission for Africa (ECA) Report: COVID-19 in Africa, OPCIT, page 13 for details on how the $100 billion would be spent

building and strengthening systems "to fight corruption and accountability of flows so that finance ministers can help track fund flows to ensure these reach the most in need expeditiously."[106]

4.3 The Trend in Ethiopia

The COVID-19 pandemic has created a chilling effect on vulnerable groups, on the economy, and on developing regional states (DRs) of Ethiopia. The UN assessment of the socioeconomic impact of COVID-19 is summarized in the following chart.

Most Impacted Groups, Sectors, and Geographic Areas – COVID 19

Workers employed in micro, small and medium size enterprises (MSMEs) in urban, informal, sector (manufacturing, construction, trading, retail, hospitality and tourism	Women in the urban informal sectors and employed in industrial parks Children of school-going age who are from poor, food-insecure households
Workers in industrial parks who are already laid off or in danger of losing their jobs	Particularly vulnerable, especially in urban informal settlements and slums
Farmers/pastoralists and households in areas at-risk of increasing food insecurity	Groups with specific vulnerabilities (persons living with HIV/AIDS (PLWHA) persons with disabilities (PWDs), older persons, the homeless)

---

[106] ECA, 13.

Frontline health system workers	IDPs, refugees, returnees, and returning migrants
Urban informal settlement and slum areas	MSMEs in supply chains in construction, manufacturing, agroindustry, hospitality, tourism, and retail
developing regional states (DRs): Afar, Benishangul-Gumuz, Gambella, Somali	MSMEs in supply chains for exports as well as well as production and marketing of critical food crops

Source: Socio-Economic Impact of COVID-19 in Ethiopia, UN, Addis Ababa, May 2020

The COVID-19 virus, which has prompted school closures, has also affected school-age children. Children from poor, food-insecure households are disadvantaged in two ways. First, they are not learning at home, while children from affluent families are learning. This creates a learning gap between children from poor and affluent households. Second, schoolchildren from poor households are missing out on school meals as schools are closed. According to UNICEF, "disrupted schooling and early childhood nutrition will have a disproportionate impact on poor families, limiting their human capital development and future earning potential."[107]

Table 36 (below) shows that 26,088,745 school-age children have been affected by the COVID crisis due to school closures.

[107] "Socio-economic impacts of COVID-19 Update," UNICEF Ethiopia, May 14, 2020, 4. Retrieved from: https://www.unicef.org/ethiopia/media/3056/file/Socio-economic%20impacts%20of%20COVID-19.pdf.

Table 36 Number of Children affected by COVID crisis due to school closure

Level	Male	Female	Total
Pre-Primary	1,676,156	1,546,097	3,222,253
Primary	10,654,351	9,392,006	20,046,357
Secondary	1,526,653	1,293,482	2,820,135
Grand Total			26,088,745

Source: Socio-economic impacts of COVID-19 Update, UNICEF Ethiopia, May 14, 2020, 4,

How is the country tackling the virus?

As a developing country, Ethiopia faces a challenge. Providing basic needs and health services for the poor and the homeless, for population living in overcrowded and slum areas, and for all the citizens is a major challenge. That is why the country is mobilizing domestic resources and international assistance.

So far, it has secured assistance from the International Monetary Fund (IMF) in the amount of US$411 million[108] under the Rapid Financing Instrument. As of May 8, 2020, USAID has committed over US$37 million[109] for COVID-19 response. The World Bank provided a US$125 million grant and US$125 million in credit.[110] The European Union shipped "nearly five million items of protective equipment—including 3.5 million

---

[108] IMF News, April 30, 2020. Retrieved from: www.imf.org.

[109] USAID News, May 8, 2020. Retrieved from: usaid.gov.

[110] World Bank News, June 17, 2020. Retrieved from https://www.worldbank.org/.

surgical masks, 35,000 face shields, 700,000 disposable respirator masks and 7,000 protective gowns."[111]

5. Summary

This chapter highlighted the impact of corruption and COVID-19 on economic growth and the poor. The findings underline that most studies on corruption demonstrate that corruption is anti-growth, which disproportionally affects the poor. The comparative assessment on corruption (for 2020) identifies Denmark, New Zealand, Finland, Singapore, Sweden, Switzerland, and Norway as the least corrupt countries. Somalia, Syria, South Sudan, Yemen, and North Korea are the most corrupt countries. According to the 2019 "Bribery Risk Matrix", Ethiopia, ranking 176th out of 200 countries with a risk score of 71, is listed as a high-risk country for bribery.

The chapter also addressed the impact of the pandemic on the poor. According to the UN, it is estimated that the pandemic will push 71 million people back into extreme poverty. In the context of Ethiopia, food prices escalating by 25 percent are expected to rapidly increase due to expected food shortages. This means that poor individuals and families would find it difficult to put food on the table. UNICEF estimates that "between 0.4–1,2 million additional people, about half of which are children, can enter into poverty." As of April 21, 2021, the number of COVID case in Ethiopia has reached 287,184 with 4,452 deaths.[112]

---

[111] European Commission News, Sept 1, 2020. Retrieved from: ec.europa.eu.

[112] World Health Organization. Retrieved from: https://covid19.who.int/region/afro/country/et

CHAPTER VI

Poverty, Employment, and Unemployment: The Global Perspective and the Ethiopian Situation

1. Introduction

This chapter starts with an overview of global poverty and poverty trends in Ethiopia. The global Multidimensional Poverty Index will also be included in the discussion to clarify the framework of poverty measurement. Then the chapter focuses on employment and unemployment trends at the global level and in Ethiopia.

Finally, the overall assessment of the chapter will provide a better picture in terms of understanding the labor market situation and poverty trend in Ethiopia to propose practical recommendations.

2. Poverty: Definition and Measurement

"Poverty entails more than the lack of income and productive resources to ensure sustainable livelihoods. Its manifestations include hunger and malnutrition, limited access to education and other basic services, social discrimination, and exclusion, as well as the lack of participation in decision-making."[113]

Measurement of Multidimensional Poverty

The global Multidimensional Poverty Index[114] is based on three dimensions: health, education, and standard of living (equally weighted), and ten indicators listed below:

a. nutrition deprivation of a household member,

b. child mortality (if a child has died),

c. years of schooling (if no family member has completed 5 years of schooling),

d. school attendance (if a child is not attending school at the age of grade eight completion),

e. deprived, if cooking with dung, wood, or charcoal,

f. deprived, if people do not have sanitation by Millennium Development Goals (MDGs) definition,

g. deprived, if not having safe drinking water,

h. deprived, if walking more than 30 minutes to obtain it, not having electricity,

i. deprived, not having shelter or a place to live, and

j. deprived, not owning more than one of a set of assets, which are radio television, telephone, bicycle, motorcycle, and refrigerator.

---

[113] United Nations. Retrieved from https://www.un.org/en/sections/issues-depth/poverty/

[114] UNDP, The 2019 Global Multidimensional Poverty Index (MPI). Retrieved from: http://hdr.undp.org/en/2019-MPI

Structure of the global Multidimensional Poverty Index

D	Health	
I		Nutrition
M		Child mortality
E		
N	Education	
S		Years of schooling
I		School attendance
O		
N	Standard of living	
S		Cooking fuel
		Sanitation
		Drinking water
		Electricity
		Housing
		Assets

Source: UNDP, Global Multidimensional Poverty Index, 3. thtttp://hdr.
undp.org/sites/default/files/mpi 2019 publication.pdf

3. Attempts to Reduce Global Poverty

The development strategy of the1950s and 1960s gave priority
to economic growth. Then, with a recognition that growth
did not alleviate poverty, the 1970s and 1980s development
strategies focused on basic needs, stabilization, and adjustment
policies. However, the global economic problem of the 1970s
and 1980s "cast a shadow over the Second (1971–1980) and
Third (1981–1990) United Nations Development Decade, and

the deteriorating economic situation led to a focus on short-term policies at the expense of long-term development goals."[115]

Millennium Development Goals (MDGs) also have not worked as planned, because "the progress on poverty eradication has been slow and uneven" (UN Development Strategy Beyond 2015). Therefore, the UN, in collaboration with member nations, set 17 goals in 2015, to be achieved by 2030. One of the goals is to eradicate poverty. The goal is ambitious. And achieving the goal remains a huge task for poor countries that are afflicted by domestic tensions and conflicts.

How many people in the world are poor?

According to the World Bank's most recent estimates, in 2015, 10 percent of the world's population, or 735 million people, lived on less than $1.90 a day. Table 37 (below) shows poverty head count ratio and the number of poor people grouped regionally.

From the table, we see that the headcount ratio increased from 2.6% to 5% between 2013 and 2015 for the Middle East and North Africa. However, for the rest of the regions, the ratio decreased slightly. As for the regional distribution of poverty, sub-Saharan Africa houses 56% of the global poor population.

---

[115] UN/DESA Policy Brief #53: "Reflection on development policy in the 1970s and 1980s," August 25, 2017, p.1 Retrieved from: https://www.un.org/development/desa/dpad/publication/policy-brief-53-reflection-on-development-policy-in-the-1970s-and-1980s/.

Table 37 Poverty rate of $1.90/day (in 2011 PPP)

Region	Headcount Ratio (%) 2013	2015	Number of Poor (Millions) 2013	2015
East Asia and Pacific	3.6	2.3	73.1	47.2
Latin America and the Caribbean	1.6	1.5	28	25.9
Middle East and North Africa	2.6	5	9.5	18.26
South Asia	16.2	12.4	274.5	216.4
Sub-Saharan Africa	42.5	41.4	405.1	413.3
World Total	11.2	10	804.2	735.9

Source: The World Bank, Sept 19, 2018. Poverty headcount ratio at $1.90 a day (2011 PPP) (% of population) | Data (worldbank.org)

4. Poverty Trend in Ethiopia

The World Bank's poverty assessment report on Ethiopia highlighted the reduction in poverty rate from 30% in 2011 to 24% in 2016, based on the most recently reported survey on household living.

The breakdown of poverty reduction by urban and rural areas reflects that progress was made in urban areas, with the poverty rate declining from 26% in 2011 to 15% in 2016. However, modest progress was achieved in rural areas, with poverty declining from 30% to 26% for the same periods. The report also points out that "the poorest 10% of the population did not experience any growth in income since 2005. As a result, poor people in 2016 were on average poorer than they were in

2005."[116] Child poverty is also pervasive. UNICEF reports that "nearly 36 million children in Ethiopia are poor and lack access to basic social services" (UNICEF, Jan. 7, 2019).

The World Bank's findings on the impact of economic growth on poverty reduction in eight countries (Ethiopia, Vietnam, Uganda, Ghana, Bangladesh, Kenya, Rwanda, and Zambia) show that economic growth has markedly contributed to poverty reduction in six of the eight countries. However, for Ethiopia and Zambia, economic growth barely contributed to poverty reduction.[117]

As the problem of poverty has taken global stage, Ethiopia has been selected by the United Nations as one of the fifty countries charged with the responsibility of providing data for the preparation of the 2030 Sustainable Development Goals (SDGs). Poverty eradication is one of the main goals.[118] This ambitious agenda of SDGs is driven by a justified cause. Poverty should be eradicated. However, the ongoing coronavirus has become the harbinger for a gloomy economy and, consequently, turning the clock back on poverty reduction goals. The World Bank estimates (based on the findings from 45 out of 48 sub-

---

[116] The World Bank, "Ethiopia Poverty Assessment: Poverty Rate Declines, Despite Challenges" (April 2020). Retrieved from: https://www.worldbank.org/en/country/ethiopia/publication/ethiopia-poverty-assessment-poverty-rate-declines-despite-challenges.

[117] See World Bank, "Special Topic: Poverty & Household Welfare in Ethiopia, 2011–2016," 51, figure B2.4.2 (growth- elasticity of poverty, 2005-2015). Retrieved from: http://documents1.worldbank.org/curated/en/432421554200542956/pdf/Special-Topic-Poverty-and-Ho.

[118] "Accelerating the Implementation of the 2030 agenda in Ethiopia," National Plan Commission Addis Ababa, April 2018. Retrieved from: https://www.un.org/development/desa/dspd/wp-content/uploads/sites/22/2018/05/4-1.pdf

Saharan African countries) poverty reduction momentum would slow down by five years (World Bank, Poverty and Equity, May 2020–Nov. 2020).

Breaking away from poverty and inequality requires programs that focus on the creation of decent work. And it is evident that unemployment has become a vexing problem, with less developed countries bearing the burden. The International Labor Organization (ILO), with its World Employment Program; the United Nations Economic, Scientific, and Cultural Organization (UNESCO), with its educational policy; the International Monetary Fund (IMF), through its adjustment program; and the World Bank have attempted to address poverty. However, the attempts have not solved poverty and the unemployment problem.

The ensuing paragraphs assess the global picture of employment, unemployment, and labor underutilization. Then, employment and underemployment theories will be discussed. Finally, the chapter focuses on Ethiopia's unemployment situation and provides strategies for curbing the problem.

"Breaking the cycle of poverty involves full employment and decent work. This has been a major thrust of the ILO approach. Evidence shows that decent and productive jobs, sustainable enterprises, and economic transformation play a key role in reducing poverty."[119]

The key to poverty reduction is to create the conditions for the poor and the unemployed so that they can participate in the economy and fulfill a set of interwoven goals. It means that

---

[119] ILO. Retrieved from: http://ilo.org/global/topics/poverty/lang--en/index.htm

when people are provided with the opportunity to be gainfully employed, they earn income, contribute to economic growth, and fulfill a sense of purpose in life, a realization of social need to work. And job creation satisfies an important human rights issue.

In his article, "Employment, social justice and societal well-being," Joseph Stiglitz "proposes that the purpose of economic activity is to improve the well-being of individuals." Stiglitz also "blames the fact that neoclassical economics treats labor like a commodity," and suggests that governments and the international community "ensure that development does not become merely a matter of capital accumulation."[120]

5. The Global Picture: Employment and Unemployment

According to the ILO[121], the global working age population was estimated at 5.7 billion for 2019. Out of which, 3.5 billion (57%) were employed, and 2.3 billion people (39%) were out of the labor force, 188 million people were unemployed, 165 million people were underemployed, and 119 million people were marginally attached to the labor force. The total labor underutilization (473 million) is more than twice as high as unemployment (188 million).

The potential labor force of 119 million (25%), includes people expressing interest in a job but not currently available for a job. Youth working age population (15–24 years) was estimated at 1.2 billion, out of which 429 million (36%) are employed; 267

---

[120] *International Labor Review* (Vol. 141, No. 1–2), 2002. Retrieved from: https://eds.b.ebscohost.com/eds/pdfviewer/pdfviewer

[121] Based on ILO data included in Chart 17 (below).

million (22%) unemployed, not in education and training; and 509 million (42%) unemployed, in education and training.

The ILO report also acknowledges that access to paid work does not guarantee decent working condition "for many of the 3.3 billion employed worldwide in 2019. All too often, the lack of income or other means of financial support compels workers to engage in jobs that are informal, offer low pay and provide little or no access to social protection and rights at work."[122]

The following chart provides the global picture of employment, unemployment, and labor underutilization.

Chart 17 Global overview of access to employment and labor underutilization, 2019		
	Working age population, 5.7 billion	
Employed 3.5 billion (57%)		Out of labor force 2.3 billion (39%)
Total labor underutilization 473 million		
Time related underemployment 165 million (35%)	Unemployed 188 million (40%)	Potential labor force 119 million (25%)

[122] World Population Review. ILO. World Employment and Social Outlook-Trends 2020, 19. Retrieved from: https://worldpopulationreview.com/country-rankings/unemployment-by-country.

	Youth working age population (15-24 years) 1.2 billion		
Youth in employment 429 million (36%)	Youth in education or training (not employed): 509 million (42%)	Youth not in employment, education	
		and training	
		267	
		million (22%)	

Source: ILO, World Employment and Social Outlook-Trends 2020, 19

6. Employment Theories

Employment theories vault back to the era of classical economists. The economic doctrine of classical economists was laissez-faire, maximum competition, and free trade. Adam Smith advocated division of labor. He used "the pin maker example to advance his theory that the division of labor results in productivity improvements."[123]

The traditional competitive full-employment model provides little insight in the context of developing countries. Wages are not flexible downward, and firms "may not be able to cut wages because of wage contracts and the legal minimum wage, and if they fear potential problems with morale, effort, and efficiency."[124] Underemployment is also pervasive in

---

[123] Jean-Louis Peaucelle, *European Journal of the History of Economic Thought* (13:4, December 2006), 490.

[124] Campbell R.McConnell and Stanley L. Brue, *Economics: Principles, Problems and Policies* (New York: McGraw-Hill, 2002), 364.

developing countries. Therefore, the traditional model does not capture the reality of developing countries.

The Keynesian model of aggregate demand, which is based on the notion that the private economy is potentially unstable, prescribes the solution to stimulate the economy and generate jobs by increasing aggregate demand. Mainstream (Keynesian-based) economists also support discretionary fiscal and monetary policies[125] to stimulate the economy and generate jobs. However, the Keynesian model of aggregate demand is also based on the realities of advanced economies, not based on the institutional and organizational preparedness of developing countries. Developing countries also face bottlenecks, such as capital, intermediate inputs, and skilled manpower shortages. Therefore, they are not ready to respond to demand stimulus as prescribed by Keynes.

The labor transformation theory of Fei and Ranis (1964) departed from the Classical and Keynesian schools of thought. To Fei and Ranis, structural problems of developing countries have been considered, and they propose the justification for labor transformation from agriculture to industry and argue that the "process of labor reallocation must be sufficiently rapid to shift the economy's center of gravity from agricultural to the industrial sector."[126] The Clark-Fisher (1980) model of labor transformation, like that of Fei and Ranis, concentrates on the role of the modern sector to solve unemployment. And the basis for the Clark-Fisher model has stemmed from two considerations:

---

[125] McConnell and Brue, *Economics*, 368.

[126] John C.H. Fei and Gustav Ranis, *Development of the Labor Surplus Economy* (Richard D. Irwin Inc, 1964), 111–112.

First, "Income elasticity of demand for food and agricultural products is lower than it is for products of the secondary and tertiary sectors."[127] This assertion does not hold true in the context of developing countries where income elasticity of demand for food is higher while it is lower in developed countries. Second, the notion that agriculture has become the source where displaced labor force would be absorbed in industry, and then in services, is not practically applied in the case of developing countries. The reality in developing countries is that excess labor is absorbed in the service sector. Galenson (1971)[128] also confirmed that the traditional labor transformation pattern from agriculture to industry and to services is not taking place. This observation is true for Ethiopia, where the service sector comprises a larger share of employment in urban areas. The Fei-Ranis explanation of the labor absorption process from sector to sector also fails to consider rural areas as a resource base for socioeconomic development. However, the Todaro model of migration considers the role of agriculture in mitigating the unemployment problem.[129]

The issue of "unemployment" is also assessed from the point of view of population growth. All things considered, when population growth is not matched by economic growth and good policy, part of the labor force remains unemployed. Regarding developing countries, where economic growth is

[127] Clark, Colin. "The Conditions of Economic Progress," in *Pattern of Urban and Rural Population Growth* (New York: UN, 1980), 111.

[128] Walter Galenson, "The Employment Problem of the Less Developed Countries: An Introduction," in ILO, *Employment* (Geneva, 1971), 5.

[129] Michael Todaro, *Economic Development in the Third World* (Longman Inc; New York, 1986).

not catching up with population growth, Malthus's observation (geometric population growth and arithmetic food production growth) has validity. However, it is not the case in advanced economies where economic growth has become sustainable, while population growth is declining. Montana and García analyzed "Malthusianism of the 21st century" in ScienceDirect (2020) and concluded that Malthus was wrong about his prediction of food production and population growth.[130]

Employment and regional development issues have also been the concerns of development thinkers. The advocates of "growth pole" theory argue in terms of the positive contribution of economic growth from its origin to adjacent areas. The theory was advanced by Perroux, Boudeville, Hirschman, and Myrdal.[131] However, the growth strategy, which prompted fascination by development economists in the 1960s, did not materialize[132] in terms of reducing poverty.

---

[130] Borja Montano and Marcos García-López, "Malthusianism of the 21st century," SinceDirect (Volume 6, June 2020). Retrieved from: https://doi.org/10.1016/j.indic.2020.100032

[131] Jean Mayer, "Regional Employment Development: The Evolution of Theory and Practice," *International Labor Review* (vol. 123, No. 1, 1984), 18.

[132] The reasons for failures of growth pole theory are included in John B. Parr, "Growth-Pole Strategies" in "Regional Economic Planning: A Retrospective View. Part 1. Origins and Advocacy," *Urban Studies* (Vol. 36, No. 7, 1999), 1195–1215.

7. Employment, Unemployment, and Underemployment: Definition and Application

7.1 Employment

In 1944, full employment was defined "as having always more vacant posts than unemployed men."[133] The improved definition reflected "a situation in which unemployment does not exceed the minimum allowances that must be made for the effects of frictional and seasonal factors."[134]

According to the thirteenth international conference of labor statistics, which took place in Geneva in 1982, the employed comprise all persons above a specified age who during a specified brief period, either one week or one day, were in the following categories:[135] a) "at work": persons who during the reference period performed some work for wage or salary, in cash or in kind, b) "with a job but not at work": persons who, having already worked in their present job, were temporarily not at work during the reference period and had a formal attachment to their job.

A full employment strategy performs three basic functions: a) "growth function—employment is a factor of economic growth, b) an income function—employment is a form of human participation in the formation and distribution of national income, and c) a social function—employment is a form of realization of social need to work, of professional and

---

[133] *International Encyclopedia of Social Sciences* (McMillan and Free Press, 1968), 56.

[134] *Ibid.*

[135] ILO, *Yearbook of Labor Statistics, 1989–1990*, 335.

social aspirations."[136] And full employment does not mean zero unemployment, because of the prevalence of a natural rate of unemployment, which includes frictional and structural unemployment.[137]

7.2 Unemployment

Unemployment is referred to a situation in which persons available and willing to work do not find work. The stock of unemployment is measured using labor force data, which includes persons that are employed and unemployed, but actively looking for jobs. The following expression can be used to compute the rate of unemployment.

$$E_n = L_n - U_n$$

where U_n = numbers unemployed, L_n = total labor force, and E_n = numbers employed in percent. Thus, we can express unemployment as:

$$U_n/L_n = (1 - E_n/L_n) \times 100 = U_n$$

In general, there are three types of unemployment: frictional unemployment, cyclical unemployment, and structural unemployment.[138]

---

[136] M. Kabaj, "Strategy of Full employment in the Polish economy" (Excerpt), Warsaw, (Institute of Labor and Social Studies), in *Employment, Wages and Productivity in Eastern Europe* (Rapallo, Sept.18–20, 1978), 684.

[137] Karl E. Case and Ray C. Fair, *Principles of Economics* (New Jersey: Prentice Hall, 2002), 423.

[138] Case and Fair, *Principles of Economics*.

7.2.1 Frictional Unemployment

Frictional unemployment is "caused by workers voluntarily changing jobs and by temporary layoffs; unemployed workers between jobs."[139]

7.2.2 Cyclical Unemployment

Cyclical unemployment emanates from business cycle fluctuations. In other words, cyclical unemployment is triggered by a decline in aggregate demand. This type of unemployment was overwhelming during the Great Depression of the 1930s.[140]

7.2.3 Structural Unemployment

Structural unemployment prevails in three phases. First, workers do not have the luxury of moving into other sectors to find jobs as preferred; second, the unemployment rate exceeds available jobs in the sectors; and third, demand shortages for certain skills prevail due to changes in technology or changes in demand, prompting layoffs.

The implication of unemployment "at the national level is that output is lost, and resources are underutilized. For individuals, income is lost, and household consumption levels are reduced."[141] And unemployment hits hard those in developing countries. According to ILO, "seventy-five percent

---

[139] McConnell and Brue, *Economics*.

[140] Robert J. Samuelson, "Revisiting the Great Depression: the role of the welfare state in today's economic crisis recalls the part played by the gold standard in the calamitous 1930s," *The Wilson Quarterly* (03633276, Vol. 36, Issue 1, 2020).

[141] K.G. Night, *Unemployment: An Economic Analysis* (London: Mackays of Chatman Ltd., 1987), 17.

of the 150 million people unemployed around the world lack any unemployment insurance protection."[142]

7.3 Underemployment

Underemployment reflects a situation where employees are only partially engaged in economic or social development activities. According to Myrdal, underemployment has various synonyms like "hidden," "latent," "potential," "concealed," and "invisible" unemployment. These nuances reflect a situation in which the labor force, engaged in economic activity is "idle during a part of the day, week, month and a year, or if working is unproductive."[143] The ILO definition of underemployment also reflects underutilization of the productive capacity of persons in employment, which can be expressed in the following forms: a) time-related—when the hours of work of an employed person are insufficient, b) skill-related—when there is a mismatch between skills and work performed, and c) income-related— underemployed people earn low income relative to their skills and qualifications.

7.3.1 Estimating Underemployment

Underemployment can be estimated with the availability of the following information: a) the volume of yearly production of a commodity (Y) or the amount of land and other resources to be used are known, b) the number of employees who would

---

[142] ILO Press Release June 21, 2000. Retrieved from: https://www.ilo.org/global/about-the-ilo/newsroom/news/WCMS_007901/lang--en/index.htm.

[143] Gunnar Myrdal, The Asian Drama, vol. III (New York: Twentieth Century Fund, 1968), 204.

be needed (L_n) to produce Y or to utilize fully if all worked full-time with "reasonable efficiency" are determined, and c) the number of workers who participate (L) in production are known; $L - L_n$ represents surplus labor; then $(L - L_n)/L$ becomes the rate of underemployment.[144]

Table 38 (below) illustrates time-related underemployment and composite rate of labor underutilization by rural/urban setting.

Table 38 Time-related and composite rate underemployment

Income Group	Demography Group	Time related underemployment		Composite rate underemployment	
		Urban	Rural	Urban	Rural
World	Total	4.1	6.1	13.8	12.3
	Female	4.7	6.8	16	13.8
	Male	3.6	5.7	2.2	11.5
	Youth	5.9	5.8	28.8	23.7
Low Income	Total	10.8	14.4	23.4	19
	female	12.1	15.1	27.4	20.2
	Male	9.7	13.7	20	18
	Youth	11.9	15.4	33.3	22.9
Low Middle Income	Total	3.7	4.9	14.2	11
	Female	4.3	5.1	19	12.4
	Male	3.4	4.8	11.9	10.4
	Youth	5.1	6.4	31.7	24.9
Upper Middle Income	Total	4.2	5.1	14.3	12.2
	Female	4.6	5.3	15.6	12.9
	Male	3.9	5	13.3	11.8
	Youth	5.8	6.9	29.5	23.4

---

[144] ILO, *Employment and Economic Growth* (Geneva, 1964), 12.

High Income	Total	3.1	3	10.6	9.4
	Female	3.9	4.1	12.3	11.5
	Male	2.3	2.2	9.1	7.8
	Youth	4.8	4.7	20.9	19.2

Source: ILO, World and Social Outlook Trends, 2020, 33.
<u>World Employment and Social Outlook - Trends 2020 (ilo.org)</u>

According to the data included in Table 38, low-income countries exhibit the highest time-related and composite rate of labor underutilization. The total labor underutilization ratio for low-income countries is 3.5 times higher than that for high-income countries. This means that for every underemployed person in high-income countries, there are more than three underemployed persons in low-income countries. This implies that for low-income economies, total labor underutilization triggers a reduction in output. For the underemployed, this means a reduction in income and deprivation from accessing basic needs.

This is a glaring problem in developing countries where social safety net programs are rarely available. Under such circumstances, the unemployed or the underemployed are pushed further into the cycle of poverty. In other words, when poor people cannot escape poverty, a poverty trap is created. "A poverty trap is a mechanism that makes it very difficult for people to escape poverty. A poverty trap is created when an economic system requires a significant amount of capital [in order] to earn enough to escape poverty. When individuals lack this capital, they may also find it difficult to acquire it, creating a self-reinforcing cycle of poverty."[145]

---

[145] Investopedia, <u>Poverty Trap Definition (investopedia.com).</u>

8. Employment, Labor Force, and Unemployment in Ethiopia

8.1 Employment

Total employment in Ethiopia (for ages 15+) is estimated at 53,849,060. Male employment accounts for 54%; female employment accounts for 46%.

Table 39 Employment in Ethiopia ('000) (15+), 2020

15+	Employment
Male	28,958.65
Female	24,890.40
Total	53,849.05

Source: ILO Stat Data Base, 2020
ILOSTAT data tools to find and download labour statistics

Chart 18 Ethiopia – Employment (,000) (15+), 2020

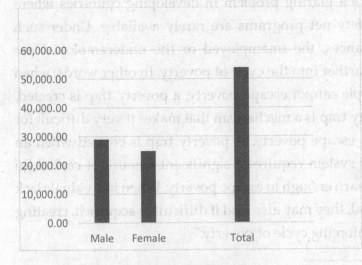

Chart created by author based on ILO data.

The total employment for ages 25+ is estimated at 36,885,650. The proportion of employment for male (54%), and female (46%) for this age group reflects a similar pattern to those included in the 15+ age category.

Table 40 Employment (,000) in Ethiopia (25+), 2020

25+	Employment
Male	19,908.30
Female	16,977.35
Total	36,885.65

Source: ILO Stat Database, 2020.
ILOSTAT data tools to find and download labour statistics.

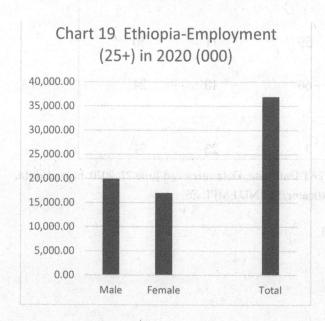

Chart 19 Ethiopia-Employment (25+) in 2020 (000)

Chart created by author based on ILO data. ILOSTAT data tools to find and download labour statistics

Table 41 (below) shows the share of employment by major economic sectors for low-income countries (including Ethiopia) and high-income countries. For low-income countries, agriculture provides the bulk of employment, followed by services and industry. For Ethiopia, agriculture accounts for 66% of total employment, the service sector accounts for 24%, and industry's share accounts for 10%. However, for high-income countries, the service sector provides the largest share of employment (74%), while agriculture generates only 3% of the total employment.

Table 41 Employment by Economic Sectors (2019) (%)

Economies	Agriculture	Industry	Services
Low-Income (average)	59	11	30
Ethiopia	66	10	24
High-Income (average)	3	23	74

Source: ILO, ILOSTAT Database. Data retrieved June 21, 2020. https://data.worldbank.org/indicator/SL.IND.EMPL.ZS.

Chart 20 Employment by Economic Sectors (2019) %

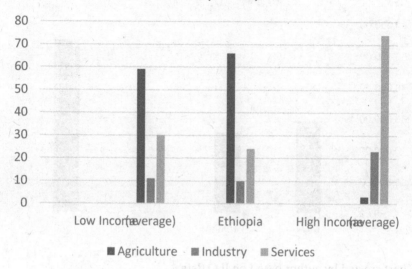

Chart created by author based on ILO data.

8.2 Labor Force

The labor force includes those within the age brackets (16–65) that are employed and those who are actively looking for jobs. Ethiopia's labor force (15+ years) is estimated at 54,994,011. The male labor force accounts for 53%, and the female labor force comprises 47%.

Table 42 Labor Force (15+) in 2019 (,000)

15+	Labor Force
Male	29,396.44
Female	25,597.67
Total	54,994.11

ILOSTAT data tools to find and download labour statistics.

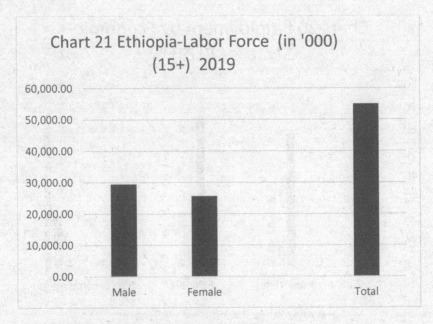

Chart 21 Ethiopia-Labor Force (in '000) (15+) 2019

Chart created by author based on ILO data.

Ethiopia's labor force (25+ years) is estimated at 37,459,922. The male labor force accounts for 54%, and the female labor force comprises 46%.

Table 43 Ethiopia- Labor Force 25+ (,000)

25+	Labor Force
Male	20,124.65
Female	17,335.27
Total	37,459.92

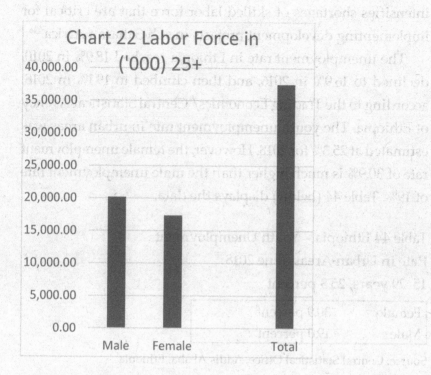

Chart 22 Labor Force in ('000) 25+

Source: ILO, Labor force by sex and age, ILO model estimates, July 2019. Chart created by author based on ILO model estimates.

8.3 Unemployment

The low level of socioeconomic development in Ethiopia is the root cause to the problem of unemployment. Open unemployment is pervasive in urban areas, mostly affecting the young population. This problem is compounded by an influx of migrants to the city. Another pressing problem which accentuates urban unemployment in developing countries is that the school system does not provide training based on the manpower requirements of the economy. This situation intensifies shortages of skilled labor force that are critical for implementing development projects in sub-Saharan Africa.[146]

The unemployment rate in Ethiopia reached 18.9% in 2010, declined to 16.9% in 2016, and then climbed to 19.1% in 2018, according to the Trading Economics/ Central Statistical Agency of Ethiopia. The youth unemployment rate in urban areas was estimated at 25.3% for 2018. However, the female unemployment rate of 30.9% is much higher than the male unemployment rate of 19%. Table 44 (below) displays the data.

Table 44 Ethiopia – Youth Unemployment
Rate in Urban Areas, June 2018
15–29 years, 25.3 percent

| Female | 30.9 percent |
| Male | 19.0 percent |

Source: Central Statistical Office, Addis Ababa, Ethiopia

What is the impact of unemployment on
the society and on the economy?

Rampant unemploymet implies loss of earnings for the unemployed, which can prompt social unrest, paving the way for regime change. The economic implication of unemployment is reduction in total output, which further exacerbates the unemployment problem.

Arthur Okun quantified the relationship between unemployment and total output (GDP). "Okun's Law indicates that for every 1 percentage point by which the actual

---

[146] ILO, _Employment and Economic Reform: Towards a Strategy for the Sudan_ (JASPA, 1986), 156.

unemployment rate exceeds the natural rate, a GDP gap of about 2 percent occurs."[147] However, Okun's observation, which was based on data from the 1960s, should be re-examined in the light of contemporary data. Current research on Okun's law provides validation and some concerns about its application. In the journals, *Open Economies* Review,[148] and in *Review of Development Economics*,[149] the research findings support Okun's Law. However, in the journal, *Structural Change and Economics Dynamics*, the research findings underline the concerns about the application of Okun's Law.[150] The reson is that while Okun's Law "rests on the idea that the rate of unemployment is a reliable indicator of labor and capacity underutilization, the assumption is questionable in some particular historical phases, such as the one the American economy has recently experienced ... and that the very low unemployment rates recorded in the U.S.A. in the late 2010s do not imply that the economy was actually at full employment (or even beyond), but rather masked some relevant underutilization of labor, that would be reflected both in low participation rates and in short average working hours."[151]

---

[147] McConnell and Brue, *Economics*, 143.

[148] Gonzalez, Prieto and Others, "What Lies Beneath? A Sub-National Look at Okun's Law in the United States," *Open Economies Review* (vol. 29, iss. 4, Sept. 2018) 835–352.

[149] Xiaoguang Liu et al., "A generalized Okun's Law: Uncovering the Myths of China's Labour market Resilience," *Review of Development Economics* (vol. 22, iss. 3, August 2018), 1195–1216.

[150] Claudia Fontanari et al., "Potential Output in Theory and Practice: A Revision and Update of Okun's Original Method," in *Structural Change and Economic Dynamics* (Sept. 2020) 54: 247–266.

[151] Fontanari et al., "Potential Output," 257–258.

9. Informal Sector Jobs

"Informal employment includes own-account workers outside the formal sector, contributing family workers, employers, and members of producers' cooperatives in the informal sector, and employees without formal contracts."[152]

According to the 2016 data (included in Chart 23 below), the informal sector of the economy generated about 61% of employment worldwide. However, for developing economies, including Ethiopia, 90% of jobs were created in the informal sector, out of which nonagricultural employment accounted for 73%.

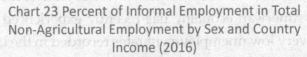

Chart 23 Percent of Informal Employment in Total Non-Agricultural Employment by Sex and Country Income (2016)

Source: Bonnet, Florence, Joann Vanek and Martha Chen. 2019. Women and Men in the Informal Economy – A Statistical Brief. Manchester, UK: WIEGO. Retrieved from: https://www.wiego.org/publications/women-and-men-informal-economy-statistical-brief

---

[152] ILO, https://ilostat.ilo.org/topics/informality/.

Most workers in developed economies participate in the formal sector of the economy, and they are guaranteed to earn "basic remuneration that is not directly dependent upon the revenue of the unit for which they work."[153] Again, to emphasize, most workers in developing countries, including Ethiopia, who are engaged in the informal sector of the economy do not have guaranteed basic remuneration. This means that they become victims of labor market fluctuations.

The following table and chart provide comparative data on the share of wage and salaried workers in total employment. For Ethiopia and sub-Saharan Africa, wage and salaried workers account for 13.7% and 24% of the total employment, respectively. However, for developed countries, more than 80% of workers are wage and salaried employees.

Table 45 Wage and Salaried Workers, Total (%of total)

Geographical Area	Percent
North America	92.9
Europe & Central Asia	82.7
European Union	84.9
Middle East & North Africa	71.2
Latin America & Caribbean	62.5

---

[153] World Bank, Oct. 26, 2020.

East Asia & Pacific	55.3
Sub-Saharan Africa	24
(Ethiopia)	13.7

Source: World Bank Modeled ILO Estimate), 2020. Retrieved from: https://data.worldbank.org/indicator/SL.EMP.WORK.ZS

Chart 24 Wage and Salaried Workers (% of total)

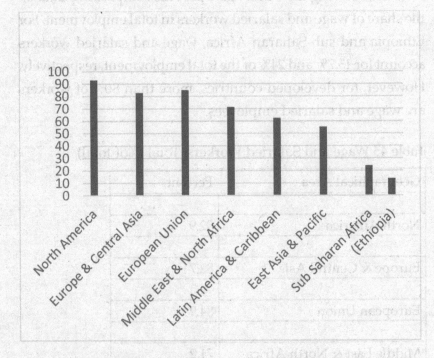

Chart created by author based on World Bank data, 2020.

10. Summary

Past development strategies did not alleviate poverty. In 2015, 10 percent of the world's population lived on less than $1.90 a day.

Millennium Development Goals (MDGs) of eradicating poverty were slow. As a result, the UN has set the goal of eradicating poverty by 2030. However, achieving the goal remains questionable for poor countries afflicted by domestic tensions and conflicts. The COVID-19 pandemic has also become the harbinger in slowing progress. The World Bank estimates that poverty reduction momentum would slow down by five years.

To eradicate poverty, the starting point is to design development programs aimed at creating decent work, which is an important human rights issue. According to the International Labor Organization (ILO), in 2019, 2.3 billion people (39 percent) were out of the labor force, 118 million people were unemployed, and 119 million people were underemployed.

The unemployment rate in Ethiopia was estimated at 19.1% in 2018. Youth unemployment rate in urban areas (for 15–29 years) accounts for 25.3%. However, the female unemployment rate of 30.9% is much higher than the male unemployment rate of 19%.

Wage and salaried workers comprise 13.7% of the total employment in Ethiopia. The share of wage and salaried workers is 24% in sub-Saharan Africa. In developed countries, salaried workers account for more than 80% of the total employment. The sad fact of the matter is that workers who are engaged in the informal sector of the economy in developing countries, including Ethiopia, do not have guaranteed basic remuneration. Consequently, they become victims of labor market fluctuations.

CHAPTER VII

Summary and Recommendations

Summary

The book addresses the prevalence of inequality and poverty in Ethiopia and suggests recommendations. The first chapter provides country background information, population, political structure, and the economy. The second chapter focuses on income distribution, household expenditure, cost of living, health, housing, and education inequalities. The highlights from the two chapters are summarized as follows:

Ethiopia is an ancient independent country located in the horn of Africa, with a land area of 386,102 square miles. The capital city, Addis Ababa, hosts international headquarters, notably, the Economic Commission for Africa (ECA) and the Organization of African Unity (OAU). Ethiopia is also the second most populous country in Africa, and twelfth in the world, with a total population of 114.96 million, out of which the female population comprises 49.7%, and the male population accounts for 50.3%. The young population (15–24 years) is estimated at 22%

of the total population. The share of urban population is 21%; the rural population accounts for 79% of the total population. The share of urban population is expected to increase with increase in the number of people migrating to urban areas.

In 2018, Ethiopia became the fastest growing economy in Africa with a GDP growth rate of 8.5%. In 2019, the country's GDP was estimated at US$96.1 billion. With a per capita income of US$857, Ethiopia is among the poorest eleven countries in the world.

For Ethiopians, life expectancy is sixty-six years, because most people are remotely connected to quality healthcare and better nutrition. Societies in developed countries live longer, with a life expectancy of eighty years. Maternal mortality rate in Ethiopia is 400 (per 100,000 live births) while it is 2 in Italy, 4 in Sweden, and 5 in Germany. For Ethiopia, there is one physician for 10,000 people. In Germany, there is one physician for about 238 people.

In primary school enrollment, Ethiopia ranks 110th, and in adult literacy, it ranks157[th] in the world. There is one teacher for fifty-five students in primary schools, which implies that primary schools in Ethiopia are underfunded. On the other hand, for developed countries, there is one teacher for eleven students. This means that a teacher in a developed country has ample opportunity to monitor the performance of students and provide individualized assistance, when needed.

Income held by the fourth 20% of Ethiopians declined from 21.3% in 2010 to 20.6% in 2015. On the contrary, income held by the highest 20% increased from 41.7% to 46.7% during the same period.

Ethiopia is also confronted by inflation. Food inflation increased to 25.9% during the month of April 2020. Globally,

Ethiopia ranks sixth in food inflation. Venezuela and Zimbabwe rank first and second, respectively.

The housing shortage is another pressing problem Ethiopia is facing. The annual demand for housing (655,800 units) by far exceeds the housing supply of 165,000 units. This housing shortage excludes the urban poor because the market caters to wealthy individuals and to those who provide collateral.

With respect to international trade, Ethiopia's major trading partners are the United States, Saudi Arabia, Germany, Switzerland, and China. Foreign trade accounts for 29% of the country's GDP, with a negative trade balance of $12.4 billion.

Chapter three is devoted to the assessment of Ethiopia's development efforts that have taken place between 1960 and 2020. The highlights from the chapter are summarized below.

The development attempts of the 1960s to early 1970s were designed to break away from poverty. Investment priorities focused on infrastructure, industry, and agriculture. This development approach mirrored the development doctrines of the 1950s, where growth focused on the achievement of physical targets. However, the achievements of the plans were low. The average growth rate in agriculture did not exceed 2% per year, which was less than the population growth rate of 2.3%. The 1970s also witnessed unrest and a regime change in Ethiopia. However, the socioeconomic development plan of the country continued with the establishment of the Office of National Committee for Central Planning (ONCCP) in 1979.

The 1980s development strategy focused on three major objectives: a) ensuring sufficient supply of goods and services, b) increasing foreign exchange earnings, and c) starting the eradication of deep-seated social problems, such as unemployment and illiteracy. Then the Ten-Year Perspective Plan (TYPP) (1983/84-1993/94) was rolled out with the objective of achieving an overall GDP growth rate of 6.5%. However, the implementation of the Five-Year Plan (of the TYPP) demonstrated shortfalls. Agriculture suffered a series of droughts, reaching the apex in 1985. And the 1980s ended with an average GDP growth rate of 1.4%, which was incompatible with the labor force growth rate of 2.9%. The planned employment target of 758,000 also remained far from being achieved.

Development plans continued in the 1990s. The Sustainable Development and Poverty Reduction Program (SDPRP) took place during 1992/1993–1999/2000. At the end of the program (2004/2005), GDP growth rate increased by 5.9%, short of the expected target of 7%. However, poverty head count ratio decreased from the 1999 level of 44.2% to 38.7% in 2004. Then the Ethiopian government rolled out the "Plan for Accelerated and Sustainable Development to End Poverty" (PASDEP) during 2005/2006–2009/2010. The result of the plan showed successful implementation. Growth targets were achieved. The average GDP growth rate of 11% exceeded the base GDP growth rate of 7%.

Following the PASDEP, the first Growth Transformation Plan (GTPI) took place between 2010/2011 and 2014/2015. At the end of the plan period, GDP growth rate increased by 10%. The economic growth rate of Ethiopia also surpassed regional and low-income averages over the past decade. Poverty head count decreased from the 2010 level of 29.6% to 23.5% in 2015. However, the poorest 10% of the population did not experience growth since 2005. As a result, poor people in 2016 were poorer than the poor in 2005.

The Second Growth Transformation Plan (GTPII)

(2015/2016–2019/2020) was then rolled out. The objective of the plan is to elevate Ethiopia's position to a lower-middle income country. Having met six of the eight Millennium Development Goals (MDGs), Ethiopia is bent on accelerating the implementation of the 2030 Sustainable Development Goals.

Chapter four focused on the impact of the environment on the poor. The findings of the chapter highlight that pollution is a global concern. Major polluters are the world's richest 1 percent. However, most air pollution–linked deaths occur in developing countries where laws are weak and not applied.

The chapter also reflected on the fact that electricity (electric power) in Ethiopia is only available to 45% of the population. Therefore, most Ethiopians resort to the daily use of firewood, charcoal, or dung for cooking and heating purposes, thereby contributing to carbon gas emissions. On the positive side, however, the Grand Ethiopian Renaissance Dam, expected to be completed by 2030 will not only bridge Ethiopia's chronic electricity shortage, but it will also position the country in a trajectory to be the largest electric exporter in Africa. Additional benefits of the dam include flood mitigation and enhanced irrigation of new agricultural land. Overall, the dam will contribute to economic growth and employment opportunities.

Then the discussion focused on the impact of land property rights as an incentive to boost land productivity and reduce poverty. The findings by Steven Lawry (*Forest News*, Feb. 2015) show strong evidence about the link between land ownership (with titles or certificates) and productivity growth in five countries in Asia and in five countries in Latin America. However, in the case of Africa, just modest gains in productivity were observed. One major cause explaining the modest gains is low investment in the farming sector.

Felix Muchomba emphasized in his study[154] that the inclusion of women in land certification increased their decision-making power in terms of household production and spending.

Chapter four also underlined the impact of CO_2 emissions on the poor. According to Our One World in Data (2017), high income countries emit more pollutants. However, in high income countries, the share of population living in extreme poverty is 0.70%. For the world, CO_2 emissions per capita were estimated at 4.79 tons (*Our One World in Data, 2017*), and the global share of population living in extreme poverty was 10% in 2015, and for sub-Saharan Africa, it was 41%. For Ethiopia, CO_2 emissions per capita were estimated at 0.14 tons, and the share of population living in extreme poverty was estimated at 26.7%.

Unsafe water caused 60% to 80% of communicable diseases and 50% of the consequence of undernutrition. Unsafe water also contributes to deaths. For Ethiopia, the share of deaths from unsafe water increased from 7.14% in 1990 to 8.9% in 2017. The 2020 Environmental Performance Index (Yale Center for Environment Law & Policy, 2020) shows that Ethiopia ranks 134th out of 180 countries. Denmark ranks first, followed by Luxembourg (second), Switzerland (third), United Kingdom (fourth), France (fifth), Austria (sixth), Finland (seventh), Sweden (eighth), Norway (ninth), and Germany (tenth). The bottom ten countries include Haiti, Chad, Solomon Islands, Madagascar, Guinea, Cote d'Ivoire, Sierra Leone, Afghanistan, Myanmar, and Liberia.

---

[154] Felix Muchomba, "Evidence from Ethiopia's Land Certification," *World Development* (vol. 98, 2017).

Chapter five highlighted the impact of corruption and COVID-19 on economic growth and the poor. The findings underline that most studies on corruption demonstrate that corruption is anti-growth, which disproportionally affects the poor. The comparative assessment on corruption (for 2020) identifies Denmark, New Zealand, Finland, Singapore, Sweden, Switzerland, and Norway as the least corrupt countries. Somalia, Syria, South Sudan, Yemen, and North Korea are the most corrupt countries. According to the 2019 Bribery Risk Matrix, Ethiopia, ranking 176th out of 200 countries with a risk score of 71, is listed as a high-risk country for bribery.

The chapter also addressed the impact of the pandemic on the poor. According to the UN, it is estimated that the pandemic will push 71 million people back into extreme poverty. In the context of Ethiopia, food prices escalating by 25% are also expected to increase further due to expected food shortages. This means that poor individuals and families will find it difficult to put food on the table. UNICEF estimates that "between 0.4–1,2 million additional people, about half of which are children, can enter into poverty."

Chapter six addressed poverty, employment, and unemployment situations at the global level and in Ethiopia. The takeaways from the discussion are summarized below.

Past development strategies did not alleviate poverty. In 2015, 10 percent of the world's population lived on less than US$1.90 a day. The Millennium Development Goals (MDGs) of eradicating poverty were slow. As a result, the U.N. has set the goal of eradicating poverty by 2030. However, achieving the goal remains questionable for poor countries afflicted by domestic tensions and conflicts. The COVID-19 pandemic has also become a factor in slowing progress. The World Bank estimates that poverty reduction momentum would slow down by five years.

To eradicate poverty, the starting point is to design development programs aimed at creating decent work, which is an important human rights issue. According to the International Labor Organization (ILO), in 2019, 2.3 billion people (39%) were out of the labor force, 118 million people were unemployed, and 119 million people underemployed. The ILO also estimated, in 2020, 20% of working Ethiopian women 25 years of age and more, and 22% of working men in the same age bracket, earned below US$1.90 per day in purchasing power parity (PPP).

The chapter continued the discussion on the unemployment situation in Ethiopia. The overall unemployment rate in Ethiopia was estimated at 19.1% in 2018. Youth unemployment in urban areas (for 15–29 years) accounts for 25.3%. However, the female unemployment rate of 30.9% is much higher than the male unemployment rate of 19%.

Wage and salaried Ethiopian workers comprise 13.7% of total employment. For sub-Saharan Africa, wage and salaried workers account for 24%; for developed countries, more than 80% of workers are wage and salaried employees. The sad fact of the matter is that workers who are engaged in the informal sector of the economy in developing countries, including Ethiopia, do not have guaranteed basic remuneration. Consequently, they become victims of labor market fluctuations. Against this backdrop, the following recommendations are suggested to curb the prevalence of pervasive poverty and inequality in Ethiopia.

Recommendations

Based on the preceding chapters, it has been demonstrated that poverty is pervasive in Ethiopia. The basic cause to the problem hinges on the low level of socio-economic development in the country. So far, attempts to curbing poverty at the international and local levels have also failed to provide solutions. The ensuing discussions highlight employment generating strategies, and policies aimed at solving poverty and inequality in Ethiopia.

1. Rural and Industrial Development

1.1 Rural Development

Rural areas house 79% of the total population of Ethiopia. Thus, rural development programs should focus on employment and poverty reduction. This approach is also practical to retain the rural labor force in rural areas if there is going to be "considerable improvement in employment opportunities, income levels and distribution in the rural areas as to improve the living conditions of the people and stave off migration to urban areas."[155]

Rural development activities include agriculture, agro-industry, and services geared to facilitating the overall rural development program. Each of the activities will be assessed as follows:

---

[155] J. D. Rogers, "Employment Generation Through Rural Development: Some Policy: Considerations," Addis Ababa: ILO/JASPA Seminar paper, Oct. 14–18, 1985, 1.

1.1.1 Agriculture

The development of agriculture requires the provision of adequate and improved inputs. "If the means of production are not delivered in time for the seasonal workers ... if the supply of fertilizers and seed grains, fuel, etc., ... is late for the season, agricultural production will lag far behind the rate that could be attained with an appropriately organized supply."[156] Therefore, the beginning of agricultural development requires sufficient means of production, and once the inputs are in good supply, the next task is to focus on production and satisfy the local and the export market.

In an awareness of the market volatility of monocrop (coffee)-dependent economy, the country is bent on diversifying its agricultural products. However, more needs to be done. Undeveloped areas can be cultivated by using appropriate (required) farm inputs (fertilizer, seed, water, labor, modern farming equipment, etc.). Importantly, sustainable farming should be encouraged. Sustainable farming incorporates "environmental health, economic profitability, and social & economic equity."[157]

1.1.2 Agro-Industry

As part of the rural development strategy, agro-industry should be developed to satisfy the consumption requirements of the rural and the urban population, and then it should be

---

[156] Joszef Bognar, *Economic Policy and Planning in Developing Countries* (Akademiai Kiado, Budapest, 1975), 267.

[157] Sustainable Agriculture Research & Education Program. UC Davis. Retrieved from: https://sarep.ucdavis.edu/sustainable-ag.

ready for the export market. Job creation should also be one of the main objectives of the rural industry.

Industrial development strategies in Less Developed Countries (LDCs) in general "seem to have ignored the employment implications of alternative product mixes and production technologies, and scale and location of industrial activities."[158] This phenomenon urges the need for integration between agriculture and industry and the possible reduction in migration rate from rural to urban areas, as well as the growth in rural income. China, for example, has facilitated rural industrialization and reinforced the government's policy in mitigating rural to urban migration.[159]

Through small-scale rural industries, local or indigenous initiatives will foster maximum use of cheaper and local technology in the context of investment constraints confronting less developed countries, including Ethiopia. Therefore, rural industrialization bridges the investment gap between the modern (industrial) and the traditional (agricultural) sector.

1.1.3 Services

Activities regarded as non-farm but which support rural development include transport, marketing, road construction, and storage. So far, "the shortage of essential institutional and infrastructural support services, i.e., extension and credit, efficient storage, transportation, marketing, and distribution

---

[158] Enyinna Chta & S.V. Sethuarman, "Rural Industrialization in Third World Development Strategies: Benign Neglect?" in *Rural Small-Scale Industries and Employment in Africa and Asia* (ILO, Geneva, 1984), 2.

[159] Radha Sinha, "Rural Industrialization in China", in *Rural Small-Scale Industries and Employment in Africa and Asia* (ILO, 1984).

services, which are indispensable to the successful operation of the rural development programs,"[160] is quite noticeable. Therefore, it is crucial to invest in rural infrastructure.

The land improvement phase, for example, involves diverse activities like cleaning drainage, irrigation, providing feeder roads, etc. These and similar activities have direct employment benefit. Evidently, the final product needs to be stored and then transported. So, storage and transportation facilities should coexist; and these services must undergo qualitative changes. The development of transportation alone can spur the growth process. "Owing to the diversification and growth of agricultural production, a supply of marketable products appears in regions where the existing transport facilities are insufficient."[161] Therefore, new roads must be constructed, and vehicles should be purchased to "permit agriculture to step into the circuit of national exchange of goods. Otherwise, the effort to boost its production will fail."[162]

1.2 Industrial Development

There are currently only 63 economies in the world classed as industrialized, making up less than 20 per cent of the global population. Yet together they produce over half of the world's manufactured goods. Emerging economy China alone churns out a further 30 per cent. In startling contrast, the 47 least developed countries (LDCs), which make up 13.4 per cent of the world's population, produce less than one per cent of

[160] Rogers, "Employment Generation Through Rural Development," 4.

[161] UN Rural Organizations (Ethiopia, April 1973), 38.

[162] Bognar, *Economic Policy and Planning in Developing Countries*, 267.

manufactured goods. Other developing countries do only a little better, together producing just two per cent.[163]

In Ethiopia, the share of industry in overall GDP is about 25%, and it accounts for 9% of the modern sector jobs. Compared to youth unemployment rate of 25.3%[164] in urban areas, it is evident that industry alone is not ready to solve the problem of unemployment. Even in the current situation where industrial parks are creating jobs, "meager pay levels have contributed to low productivity and high attrition rates."[165] Therefore, agriculture and services should be ready to provide additional job opportunities.

1.2.1 *Services*

All kinds of infrastructural services that help to speed up industrial development foster job creation. Maintenance and repair; construction of industrial buildings; transportation of local inputs from agriculture are some of the services required by the industrial sector of the economy. Thus, services are deemed vital as a catalyst for industrial development. And the process of industrialization does not stop there. Goods produced need to be distributed through distribution centers, which in turn provide job opportunities for transportation workers, sales workers, accountants, clerks, and shop attendants, etc.

---

[163] UNIDO, Sept 17, 2020 https://www.unido.org/stories/what-industrialization-means-well-being--and-why-it-matters.

[164] Central Statistical Agency, Addis Ababa, Ethiopia.

[165] "A new industry in Ethiopia is creating jobs. But at what cost?" *Washington Post*, May 10, 2019. Retrieved from: https://www.washingtonpost.com/opinions/2019/05/10/new-industry-ethiopia-is-creating-jobs-what-cost/

2. Population Dynamics

The Ethiopian population is estimated at 114.96 million. The overall population growth is estimated at 2.6% per year. If this growth rate continues, the population will double in 27 years according to Rule of 70. "Rule of 70 is a method for determining the number of years it will take for some measure to double, given its annual percentage increase."[166] The labor force is estimated to reach 61 million in 2030, based on the assumption that the average labor force growth trend (2.7%) between 2010 and 2020 would continue. Appendix 4 includes the steps involved in estimating the labor force growth.

The urban population is also increasing at 4.8% per year. As things stand at present, the urban population growth would put pressure on the services rendered in urban areas, including housing, education, transportation, and health. The urban population growth also compounds the unemployment problem. Therefore, to mitigate the growing urban population, existing family planning programs should be encouraged and supported. In addition, settlement and resettlement programs need to be carried out to fulfill two tasks: a) to develop hitherto undeveloped areas, and b) to settle people from densely populated areas into sparsely populated areas. Through the application of these programs, resources can be harnessed for development, which also creates employment opportunities.

---

[166] McConnell and Brue, *Economics*.

3. Education

Education provides interwoven multidimensional benefits ranging from poverty reduction to improved nutrition, health, and well-being, leading to inequality reduction, environmental protection, and peaceful, just, and inclusive societies. The UN has recognized the importance of delivering quality education for everyone across the globe. "Quality Education" is identified as goal number four among the seventeen Sustainable Development Goals (SDGs).

A review of evidence reflects that the current educational system of Ethiopia is not aligned with the manpower requirements of the economy. "High and growing unemployment among Ethiopian university graduates, meanwhile, raises questions about the quality and relevance of academic curricula which are considered ill-suited for current labor market demands."[167] Therefore, it is crucial for the government to invest in quality education that fulfills personal, social, and economic objectives.

3.1 Education must be purpose oriented.

In addition to a host of benefits gained from education, education is the engine of economic growth. Therefore, the manpower needs of the economy should be met by education. The ongoing technical and vocational education should be encouraged, which goes with the educational plan of the country. Regarding skilled manpower shortages, it is worth expanding training centers to bridge the gap. Given the prevailing shortages of skilled professionals, the reliance on

---

[167] WENR, Education in Ethiopia, November 15, 2018. https://wenr.wes.org/2018/11/education-in-ethiopia, Stefan Trines, Research Editor, WENR.

expatriate experts continues. However, long-term training (both at home and abroad) in critical areas of shortages, short-term seminars, and on the job-training should be encouraged to mitigate the shortage of skilled manpower.

4. Healthcare

In 2018, Ethiopia spent 3.3% of its GDP on health care. However, on average, four industrialized countries (France, Germany, Switzerland, and the United States) spent 12.8% of their GDP on health care (according to World Bank data). This means that Ethiopia needs to invest more money in healthcare.

The current situation in Ethiopia reflects that health services are in short supply compared to the needs of the population. The fact that there is one physician for 10,000 people in Ethiopia is a clear indication that the country is facing acute shortages of health services. To bridge this shortage, the Ethiopian government should mobilize resources to expand healthcare access for the society free of charge. At the same time, the government should encourage private healthcare providers to invest in healthcare infrastructure and deliver healthcare services at an affordable price.

Among the seventeen UN Sustainable Development Goals (SDGs) set for 2030, goal number three is to provide access to "good health and well-being." Therefore, member nations, including Ethiopia, are required at least to show some progress regarding access to healthcare. In the best-case scenario, the expectation is to achieve the goal.

5. Housing

Access to affordable housing implies safety, peace of mind, and a better tomorrow. Homelessness is a burden for the poor; it aggravates poverty and accentuates social problems.

The Ethiopian urban population is growing rapidly (4.8% per year). And the housing demand far exceeds the available supply of housing. Therefore, the government should cater to the poor by building affordable houses and by expanding or establishing cities in rural areas to stave off rural to urban migration. The government can also encourage private companies to construct affordable houses in urban and in rural areas. Therefore, the combined effort of the government and businesses would make a huge difference in terms of mitigating housing shortages and creating job opportunities.

6. Employment Planning

Employment planning plays a significant role in redressing the mismatch between labor supply and labor demand. So far, employment planning has been considered a derivative of economic planning, and the focus has been toward the attainment of physical targets. The employment offices also play a passive role by allocating manpower only when available vacancies are reported by employers. Therefore, manpower planning should take place to address the current and future shortages of skilled manpower by providing the required training and education.

7. The Role of Employment Services

Historically, "public employment services were created essentially to counter the activities of private agents accused of acting like traffickers in human beings, and as strike breakers by the burgeoning trade union movement, the private agents were marked out for general opprobrium. Later [on], in the years immediately after the Second World War, public employment services began to justify themselves in economic terms. Although originally intended to exercise a social function, they found themselves taking on an unexpected role in the regulation of industrial production: they became the embodiment of the classical theory of the functioning of the labor market. However, the decolonization movement that began after the Second World War and became a flood in the 1960s, established the ascendancy of development economics, for which unemployment is not the result of temporary disequilibrium but the symptom of a deep seated and lasting dysfunction in the production system. Thus, in this view of things, public employment services became or came to be seen as insignificant cogs in the giant state machine devoted entirely to the development effort and the creation of jobs."[168]

However, in the current situation, the Ministry of Labor and Social Affairs and the ILO recommend the following ideas to speed up the process of job creation:

a. "build institutional and resource capacity of Public Employment Services (PES),

---

[168] Sergio Ricca, "The Changing role of public employment services," in ILO, *International Labor Review*, (vol. 127, No. 1), 1988), 19–20.

b. provide the required support to job seekers and employers,

c. strengthen the capacity of PES, to collate, store, analyze, interpret,

d. disseminate and use labor market information,

e. promote public employment services to the public, decision makers, employers as well as job seekers to create awareness and ensure service use by job seekers and employers, and

f. improve coordination among LMIS producers and users to formalize collaboration and facilitate information exchange between LMI producers and users."[169]

8. Employment Promotion Fund (EPF)

In a country such as Ethiopia, where both open and hidden unemployment coexist, the employment promotion fund (EPF) can foster the creation of jobs. Hungary, for example, used EPF[170] to mitigate unemployment. The sources of EPF can emanate from the following: a) government's investment fund, b) donations from nongovernmental and international organizations, and c) public contributions. Once the fund is secured through the above means, the next task would be to administer the fund for the purpose of creating productive jobs. The Ministry of Labor and Social Affairs can assume the responsibility in terms of administering and monitoring the EPF.

---

[169] ILO, and Ministry of Labor and Social Affairs (MoLSA), *Public Employment Services Provision and Labor Market Information Collection and Utilization – Ethiopia*, 2018, xi–xv. https://www.itcilo.org/sites/default/files/inline-files/Assessment-of-the-public-employment-services_web.pdf.

[170] On Employment Promotion and Provision for Unemployed Persons (Budapest: Ministry of Labor, Hungary, Act. IV of 1991).

The EPF can also be utilized for financing job-training to improve the participants' skills. "The target groups are often young ... but also include adults who are unemployed. Unemployed persons wishing to set up an enterprise or take over an enterprise in difficulty"[171] can do so through loanable money from EPF based on certain terms and conditions. The EPF can also be a financial source for conducting research, geared to the expansion of employment programs. The fund also serves the speedy function of public works programs,[172] which include construction of roads and bridges; soil conservation (including reforestation and other forest protection works); irrigation and water supply; low-cost housing, schools, and storage facilities.

9. The Need for a Strong Data Base for Human Resource Planning

Currently, the public sector employment data is available. However, the informal and the peasant sector employment and unemployment pictures are not available. Therefore, the data on the informal sector of the economy should be made available. To this end, the Ministry of Labor and Social Affairs, in collaboration with the Central Statistical Agency and the Planning and Development Commission can collect information, explore, and understand the real conditions workers face in the informal and peasant sector of the economy and provide financial-assistance and training for struggling workers, and for businesses.

---

[171] ILO, International Labor Review (vol. 127, No. 1, 1988), 3.

[172] ILO, International Labor Review (vol. 129, No. 2, 1990), 167.

10. The Role of Women

The International Labor Organization (ILO) acknowledges that globally, women make 77 cents for every dollar earned by men. In developing countries, including Ethiopia, women have shouldered burdensome tasks. Women also participate in the farm. More so, they carry water and wood from distant places for daily needs. At home, they are busy cooking food and looking after children. However, they are "under-represented in the decision-making categories of the labor force."[173]

As women, they have special interest in policies pertaining to "family planning, maternal delivery services and legal protection against abuse or discrimination, provision of childcare facilities, more flexible working arrangements that will enable them to fulfill their roles as mothers and members of the labor force."[174] This situation prompted a global movement and demonstration calling for women empowerment. The concern is also felt by the Ethiopian women. Indeed, gender equality is included as goal number 5 of the seventeen UN Sustainable Development Goals (SDGs) set for 2030.

Cognizant of this fact and driven by the success story of the Grameen Bank in Bangladesh, Ethiopia has already initiated microcredit through microfinance institutions (MFIs) to make a difference in the lives of poor women. In the long run, however, "improving the level of credit access in Ethiopia is beneficial for increasing the overall economic self-sufficiency

---

[173] UN, *World Economic Survey, 1990*, 200.

[174] UN. https://www.un.org/ruleoflaw.

of communities."[175] Therefore, Ethiopian women must be supported and encouraged to be direct participants in the social, economic, and political affairs of their country.

11. Application of the Rule of Law to Reduce Corruption and Poverty

"The rule of law is a principle of governance in which all persons, institutions, and entities, public and private, including the State itself, are accountable to laws that are publicly promulgated, equally enforced, and independently adjudicated, and which are consistent with international human rights norms and standards. It requires measures to ensure adherence to the principles of supremacy of the law, equality before the law, accountability to the law, fairness in the application of the law, separation of powers, participation in decision-making, legal certainty, avoidance of arbitrariness, and procedural and legal transparency."[176]

According to Transparency International, corruption targets the poor most. The World Economic Forum warns that ending poverty should start with stopping corruption. Therefore, it is recommended to apply the rule of law and protect the poor and the powerless from being exploited.

---

[175] "Credit Access in Ethiopia Growing in Rural Areas," *Borgen Magazine*, Jan. 16, 2018 Credit Access in Ethiopia Growing in Rural Areas - BORGEN (borgenmagazine.com).

[176] World Economic Forum, Jan 23, 2015. https://www.weforum.org/agenda/2015/01/want-to-end-poverty-start-with-corruption.

12. Environmental Factors

Environmental factors affect our existence. Sustainable development cannot proceed without protecting the environment. Most air pollution–linked deaths occur in developing countries where laws are not enforced. In Ethiopia, most households are exposed to carbon emissions during their daily use of firewood, charcoal, or dung for cooking and heating purposes. Unsafe water also contributes to deaths. According to *Our World in Data*, in Ethiopia, the share of deaths from unsafe water increased from 7.14% in 1990 to 8.9% in 2017.

Environmental degradation mostly affects the poor. Therefore, it is crucial to invest in cleaner technology, and to create public awareness about the importance of protecting the environment for our survival.

13. Remittance

According to Investopedia, "a remittance is a payment of money that is transferred to another party. Broadly speaking, any payment of an invoice or a bill can be called a remittance. However, the term is most often used nowadays to describe a sum of money sent by someone working abroad to his or her family back home."[177]

A remittance makes a difference for Ethiopians. It helps to fulfill a set of objectives. The UN identifies the contribution of a remittance in terms of achieving at least seven of the seventeen Sustainable Development Goals (SDGs) by 2030. The seven

---

[177] https://www.investopedia.com/terms/r/remittance.asp.

goals[178] are a) no poverty, b) zero hunger, c) good health and well-being, d) quality education, e) clean water, f) decent work and economic growth, and g) reduced inequality.

It is true that remittance helps poor families to put food on the table and access clean water. Poor families or individuals can also invest the money in new businesses and fulfil their dreams of self-sufficiency. The money also gives them a sense of freedom on how to utilize it.

At the macro level, remittances coming from North America or Europe help local banks to increase their reserves of hard currencies. Therefore, the government should encourage the flow of remittances to the country by providing incentive, such as a tax credit "to remittance service providers equal to the reduction in fees paid by remittance senders and recipients."[179] The government should also "encourage market competition in the remittances industry."[180]

14. Business Environment

Based on the World Bank's methodology of "ranking business climate," Ethiopia ranks 159th out of 190 countries. The regulatory environment also is not conducive to attracting foreign investment in Ethiopia. Therefore, the Ethiopian government should ease the regulatory restrictions to encourage and

[178] UN, "Remittances matter," New York June 17, 2019. Retrieved from: https://www.un.org/development/desa/en/news/population/remittances-matter.html.

[179] Mahmoud Mohieldin and Dilip Ratha, "How to Keep Remittances Flowing, Brookings, June 11, 2020. https://www.brookings.edu/blog/future-development/2020/06/11/how-to-keep-remittances-flowing/.

[180] Moheldin and Ratha, "How to Keep Remittances Flowing."

attract investment to stimulate economic growth and create job opportunities.

It is proven that markets allocate resources to their best alternative uses. Therefore, easing regulatory restrictions on businesses results in competition. When businesses compete, consumers have choices and preferences on how to spend their money. And as the business climate keeps on fostering competition, the government should not intervene in the marketplace. However, if the business climate stifles competition, government regulation is indispensable for the well-functioning of the economy.

15. Poverty Reduction Lessons

Appendix 5 highlights poverty reduction lessons from three countries: Brazil, China, and Norway. The common denominator for these three countries is the proof that targeted government programs make a difference in combating poverty. In Brazil and in China, organized leadership facilitated poverty reduction. Norway has endorsed inclusive development strategy and achieved an enviable standard of living. Norway is also the country that has the lowest income inequality in the world. Therefore, the success stories of these three countries can offer practical lessons for policymakers in Ethiopia.

It should be underlined that inclusive development starts with good governance. Then, development proceeds with the objective of improving the overall standard of living of the society. In the process, poverty alleviation programs should deserve a top priority. Poverty reduction (No Poverty) is also identified as the first of the seventeen Sustainable Development Goals (SDGs) of 2030.

In the end, it is evident that poverty still looms large in Ethiopia. Efforts taken to reduce poverty have just touched the tip of the iceberg. Against this background, this book has added more details about the prevalence of pervasive poverty and inequality in Ethiopia and highlighted integrated strategies to curbing the problems.

BIBLIOGRAPHY

1   "Accelerating the Implementation of the 2030 agenda in Ethiopia." National Plan Commission. Addis Ababa, April 2018. Retrieved from: https://www.un.org/development/desa/dspd/wp-content/uploads/sites/22/2018/05/4-1.pdf

2   Acemoglu, Daron and James Robinson. "Corruption Is Just a Symptom, Not the Disease." *The Wall Street Journal*, Dec. 3, 2015. Retrieved from: https://www.wsj.com/articles/corruption-is-just-a-symptom-not-the-disease-1449174010

3   Acemoglu, Daron and James Robinson. "Rents and economic development: the perspective of Why Nations Fail." *Public Choice* vol. 181, 13-28, Oct. 2019. Retrieved from: https://doi.org/10.1007/s11127-019-00645-z

4   African Wildlife Foundation. Retrieved from: https://www.awf.org/country/ethiopia

5   Alexianu, Matei. "Is green growth possible? Revisiting the Environmental Kuznets curve." Industrial Growth Center (IGC), January 2, 2019. Retrieved from: Is green growth possible? Revisiting the Environmental Kuznets curve - IGC (theigc.org)

6   "A new industry in Ethiopia is creating jobs. But at what cost?" *Washington Post*, May 10, 2019. Retrieved from: https://www.washingtonpost.com/opinions/2019/05/10/new-industry-ethiopia-is-creating-jobs-what-cost/

7   An Africa Watch Report, Sept 1991. Retrieved from: https://www.hrw.org/sites/default/files/reports/Ethiopia919.pdf

8 Bardhan, Pranab. Corruption and Development: A Review of Issues, *Journal of Economic Literature* Vol. 35, No. 3 (Sept. 1997). Retrieved from: https://www.jstor.org/stable/2729979

9 Bloomberg, July 14, 2020. Retrieved from: https://www.bloomberg.com/news/articles/2020-07-14/zimbabwe-continues-its-march- back-to-hyperinflation

10 Bognar, Jozsef. *Economic Policy and Planning in Developing Countries.* Budapest: Akademiai Kiado, 1975.

11 Bonnet, Florence, Joann Vanek and Martha Chen. *Women and Men in the Informal Economy – A Statistical Brief.* Manchester, UK: WIEGO, 2019. statistical-brief

12 Case, Karl E., and Ray C. Fair. *Principles of Economics.* New Jersey: Prentice Hall, 2002.

13 Chai, Andreas. *Household consumption patterns and the sectoral composition of growing economies: A review of the interlinkages.* Vienna: UNIDOO, 2018. Retrieved from: https://www.unido.org/api/opentext/documents/download/10166980/unido-file-10166980

14 Center for Affordable Housing Finance in Africa (CAHF), 2019. Retrieved from: http://housingfinanceafrica.org/

15 *China's success in poverty alleviation: Lessons for other Countries.* World Bank, Sept 20, 2019. Retrieved from: https://news.cgtn.com/news/2019-09-20/China-s-success-in-poverty-alleviation-Lessons-for-other-countries-K8Bg9Fsxe8/index.html

16 CIA, The World Factbook (February 2020). Retrieved from https://www.cia.gov/library/publications/the-world-factbook/geos/et.html

17 Clark, Colin. "The Conditions of Economic Progress," in Patterns of Urban and Rural Population Growth. New York: UN, 1980.

18 Cohen, John M. *Integrated Rural Development: The Ethiopian Experience and the Debate.* Motala: Motala Grafiska, 1987.

19 *Combating Corruption.* World Bank. Retrieved from: https://www.worldbank.org/en/topic/governance/brief/anti

20 Copier, Raffaella, Mauro Costantini, and Gustavo Piga. "The Role of Monitoring of Corruption in a Simple Endogenous Growth Model."

Economic Inquiry vol. 51, No. 4 (October 2013). Retrieved from: https://ideas.repec.org/a/bla/ecinqu/v51y2013i4p1972-1985.html

21 Economic Commission in Africa. "COVID-19 in Africa." Addis Ababa, April 2020. Retrieved from: https://www.uneca.org/publications/covid-19-africa protecting-lives-and-economies4

22 Economic Indicators for Ethiopia,2020. Retrieved from: https://import-   export.societegenerale.fr/en/country/ethiopia/growth-indicators

23 Encyclopedia Americana. American Corporation (vol 10), 1966.

24 Encyclopedia Britannica. Retrieved from: https://www.britannica.com/place/Ethiopia/Religion

25 "Ending Corruption to End Poverty." Transparency International, September 25, 2013. Retrieved from: https://www.transparency.org/en/news/ending-corruption-to-end-poverty

26 Ethiopia: Building on Progress: A Plan for Accelerated and Sustained Development to End Poverty (PASDEP) (2005/06–2009/10) Volume I: Ministry of Finance and Economic Development (MoFED).

27 Ethiopia's Climate-Resilient Green Economy. Federal Democratic Republic of Ethiopia, 2011. Retrieved from: file:///C:/Users/Owner/Downloads/Ethiopia%20CRGE.pdf

28 Ethiopia Demographic and Health Survey 2011. Addis Ababa, Ethiopia and Calverton, Maryland, USA: Central Statistical Agency and ICF International. Retrieved from: https://www.dhsprogram.com/pubs/pdf/FR255/FR255.pdf

29 Ethiopia's Great Run, The Growth Acceleration and How to Pace It. World Bank. Feb 2016. Retrieved from: http://documents1.worldbank.org/curated/en/693561467988949839/pdf/99399-

30 Ethiopia – Socio-economic impacts of COVID 19 update. UNICEF, May 14, 2020. Retrieved from: https://www.unicef.org/ethiopia/media/3056/file/Socio-economic%20impacts%20of%20COVID-19.pd

31 *Ethiopia – Youth Unemployment Rate in Urban Areas.* Addis Ababa: Central Statistical Office, June 2018. Retrieved from: file:///C:/Users/Owner/Downloads/Key%20Findings%202018%20UEUS.pdf

32 EPI, Yale Center for Environment Law & Policy, Yale University. Retrieved from: https://epi.yale.edu/downloads/epi2020report20200911.pdf

33 European Commission News, Sept 1, 2020. Retrieved from https://ec.europa.eu/info/news_en

34 Fei, John C. H., and Gustav Ranis. *Development of the Labor Surplus Economy*. USA: Richard D. Irwin Inc., 1964.

35 "Five stages for Poverty reduction in Brazil." *Borgen Magazine*, Feb. 23, 2018. Retrieved from: https://www.borgenmagazine.com/poverty-reduction-in-brazil/

36 Fontanari, Claudia, and others. "Potential Output in Theory and Practice; A Revision and Update of Okun's Original Method" *Structural Change and Economic Dynamics* vol. 54, C (Sept 2020).

37 Galenson, Walter. The employment Problem of the Less Developed Countries: An Introduction, in *Essays on Employment*. ILO, 1971.

38 Ginzberg, Eli and Herbert A. Smith. A Manpower strategy for Ethiopia. Addis Ababa, 1966.

39 Greenfield, David. Menelik II. Retrieved from: https://www.britannica.com/biography/Menilek-II

40 Global Partnership (June24, 2019). Retrieved from: https://www.globalpartnership.org/

41 Gonzalez, Prieto, and others, "What Lies Beneath? A Sub-National Look at Okun's Law in the United States," *Open Economies Review* (vol. 29 iss. 4), Sep. 2018.

42 Grundler, Klaus, and Niklas Potrafke. "Corruption and economic growth: New empirical Evidence." *European Journal of Political Economy* vol. 60 (2019). Retrieved from: https://ideas.repec.org/a/eee/poleco/v60y2019ics0176268019301156.html

43 "Haile Selassie: Why the African Union put up a statue." BBC News. Retrieved from: https://www.bbc.com/news/world-africa-47172020

44 Harvey, Fiona, *The Guardian*, Sept. 20, 2020. Retrieved from: https://www.theguardian.com/environment/2020/sep/21/worlds-richest-1-cause-double-co2-emissions-of-poorest-50-says-oxfam

45 "How Ethiopia achieved Millennium Development Goal 4 through multisectoral interventions: A Countdown to 2015 case study." *Lancet Global Health*, Nov. 2017. Retrieved from:https://www.thelancet.com/journals/langlo/article/PIIS2214-109X(17)30331- 5/fulltext

46 "How to Reduce Poverty: A New Lesson from Brazil for the World?" World Bank, March 22, 2014. Retrieved from: https://www.worldbank.org/en/news/feature/2014/03/22/mundo-sin-

47 International Encyclopedia of Social Sciences. New York: McMillan and Free Press, 1968.

48 ILO Press Release, June 21, 2000, Retrieved from: https://www.ilo.org/global/about-the-ilo/newsroom/news/WCMS_007901/lang--en/index.htm

49 ILO. *Statistics on Wages*. ILOSTAT 2020 estimate. Retrieved from: https://ilostat.ilo.org/topics/wages/

50 ILO. *Employment and Economic Growth*. Geneva, 1964

51 ILO. *Employment and Economic Reform: Towards a Strategy for the Sudan (JASPA)*, 1986.

52 ILO. *International Labor Review* (vol. 127, No. 1), 1988.

53 ILO. *International Labor Review* (vol. 129, No. 2), 1990.

54 ILO Stat Database, 2020. Retrieved from: https://data.worldbank.org/indicator/SL.IND.EMPL.ZS

55 ILO. *World Employment and Social Outlook – Trends 2020*. Retrieved from: https://worldpopulationreview.com/country_rankings/unemployment-by-country

56 ILO, and Ministry of Labor and Social Affairs (MoLSA). *Public Employment Services Provision and Labor Market Information Collection and Utilization – Ethiopia*, 2018, xi–xv. Retrieved from: https://www.itcilo.org/sites/default/files/inline-files/Assessment-of-the-public-employment-

57 International Monetary Fund, February 24, 2020. Retrieved from: https://www.imf.org/external/pubs/ft/fandd/basics/trade.htm

58 IMF. Staff Country Report on Economic Development in Ethiopia (No. 99/98), July 13, 1999. Retrieved from: https://www.imf.org/external/pubs/ft/scr/1999/cr9998.pdf

59 IMF News, April 30, 2020. Retrieved from: www.imf.org

60 International Rescue Committee. Addis Ababa, Oct 7, 2020. Retrieved from: https://www.rescue.org

61 Jetter, Michael. "The Intimate Link Between Income Levels and Life Expectancy: Global Evidence from 213 Years," *Social Science Quarterly*, June 1, 2019.

62 Kabaj, M. "Strategy of Full Employment in the Polish economy." *Employment, Wages and Productivity in Eastern Europe*. Rapallo, Sept.18–20, 1978.

63 Krugman, Paul. *The New York Times* (vol. 157, No. 54172). 2007.

64 Lawry, Steven. "How does land tenure affect agricultural productivity? A systematic review." *Forests News* February 24, 2015. Retrieved from: https://forestsnews.cifor.org/26908/land-tenure-reforms-africa-review?fnl=

65 Loeb, Benjamin S. "Use of Engel's Laws as a basis for predicting consumer expenditures." *Journal of Marketing* vol. 20, Issue 1 (July 1955).

66 Makoni, Munyardzi. "Air Pollution in Africa," *The Lancet*, July 2020. Retrieved from: https://www.thelancet.com/journals/lanres/article/PIIS2213-2600(20)30275-7/fulltext

67 Manpower Implications of Current Development Strategies (vol. 1), Addis Ababa, Nov. 1984.

68 Mayer, Jean. "Regional Employment Development: The Evolution of Theory and Practice." *International Labor Review* vol. 123, No. 1 (1984).

69 McConnell, Campbell R., and Stanley L. Brue. Economics: Principles, Problems and Policies. New York: McGraw-Hill, 2002.

70 Menelik II. Retrieved from: https://www.encyclopedia.com/people/history/african-history-biographies/mene:lik-ii

71 Mohieldin, Mahmoud, and Dilip Ratha. "How to keep remittances flowing." Brookings, June 11, 2020. Retrieved from:https://www.brookings.edu/blog/future-development/2020/06/11/how-to-keep-remittances-flowing/

72　Montano, Borja, and García-López, Marcos. Malthusianism of the 21st century, (Vol. 6), June 2020. Retrieved from: https://doi.org/10.1016/j. indic.2020.100032

73　Mulat, Teshome, and Eshetu Chole. *Patterns of Industrialization and Impact on Employment and incomes in African Countries: The case of Ethiopia.* Addis Ababa: JASPA, 1983.

74　Gunnar Myrdal, *The Asian Drama.* New York: Twentieth Century Fund (vol. III), 1968.

75　National Geographic, May 11, 2020. Retrieved from: Environmental Impacts of Agricultural Modifications | National Geographic Society

76　Nevin, Vahideh. *The Causal Relationship between Corruption and Poverty: A Panel Data Analysis.* January 2010. Retrieved from: file:///C:/ Users/Owner/Downloads/causality between corruption and poverty.pdf

77　Night, K.G. *Unemployment: An Economic Analysis.* London: Mackays of Chatam Ltd, 1987.

78　*On Employment Promotion and Provision for Unemployed Persons.* Budapest: Ministry of Labor, Hungary, Act. IV of 1991.

79　"Remittances matter." New York: UN, June 17, 2019. Retrieved from https://www.un.org/development/desa/en/news/population/ remittances-matter.html

80　Our World in Data, Aug. 2020. Retrieved from:https://ourworldindata. org/grapher/co-emissions-per-capita-vs-the-share-of-people-living- in-extreme-poverty

81　Our World in Data, Nov. 2019. Retrieved from: https://ourworldindata. org/water-access

82　Peaucelle Jean-Louis. *European Journal of the History of Economic Thought* vol. 13, No. 4 (December 2006). Retrieved from: http://www. tandf.co.uk/journals

83　PEW Research Center (Jan 29, 2018). Retrieved from: Remittances can be big economic assets for countries | Pew Research Center

84 PEW Research Center. February 14, 2017.Retrieved from: https://www.pewresearch.org/fact-tank/2017/02/14/african-immigrant-population-in-u-s-steadily-climbs/

85 Plumer, Brad. "You've Heard of Outsourced Jobs, but Outsourced Pollution? It's Real, and Tough to Tally Up." *The New York Times*, Sept 4, 2018.Retrieved from: https://www.nytimes.com/2018/09/04/climate/outsourcing- carbon- emissions.html

86 *Poverty and Economic Growth in Ethiopia (1995/96–2015/16)*. Addis Ababa: Planning and Development Commission, Dec. 2018.

87 *Poverty Assessment: Poverty Rate Declines Despite Challenges*. World Bank, April 2020. Retrieved from: https://www.worldbank.org/en/country/ethiopia/publication/ethiopia-poverty- assessment-poverty-rate-declines-despite-challenges

88 Ricca, Sergio, "The Changing role of public employment services." *International Labor Review* vol. 127, No. 1 (1988).

89 Rogers, J.D. "Employment Generation Through Rural Development: Some Policy Considerations." Addis Ababa: ILO/JASPA Seminar paper, Oct. 14–18, 1985.

90 Samuelson, Robert J. "Revisiting the Great Depression: the role of the welfare state," in "Today's economic crisis recalls the part played by the gold standard in the calamitous 1930s." *The Wilson Quarterly* 03633276, vol. 36, no. 1 (2020).

91 *Second Five-Year Development Plan of Ethiopia (1963–1967)*. Addis Ababa: Berhanenna Selam Printing Press, Oct 1962.

92 *Socio-Economic Impact of COVID-19 in Ethiopia*. Addis Ababa: UN, May 2020. Retrieved from: https://www.unicef.org/ethiopia/media/3056/file/Socio-economic%20impacts%20of%20COVID-19.pdf

93 *Sustainable Agriculture Research & Education Program*. UC Davis. Retrieved from: https://sarep.ucdavis.edu/sustainable-ag

94 *Tace Bribery Risk Matrix*. Retrieved from: https://www.traceinternational.org/trace-

95 The Borgen Project. How Poverty Impacts the Environment. Oct. 2, 2013. Retrieved from: https://borgenproject.org/how-poverty-impacts-the-environment/

96 *The Economics of Climate.* IMF F&D, December 2019. Retrieved from: https://www.imf.org/external/pubs/ft/fandd/2019/12/pdf/fd1219.pdf

97 *The Global Economic Outlook During the COVID-19 Pandemic: A Changing World.* World Bank, June 18, 2020.

98 *The Guardian*, July 30, 2020. Retrieved from: https://www.theguardian.com/global-development/2020/jul/30/a-dollar-for-sex-venezuelas-women-tricked-and-trafficked

99 *The Guardian*, Sept. 20, 2020. Retrieved from: https://www.theguardian.com/environment/2020/sep/21/worlds-richest-1-cause-double-co2-emissions-of-poorest-50-says-oxfam

100 *The Guardian*, July 16, 2011. Retrieved from: https://www.theguardian.com/lifeandstyle/2011/jul/17/bread-food-arab-spring

101 The Second Growth and Transformation Plan (GTP II) Midterm Review Report. Addis Ababa: National Planning Commission, June 2018.

102 *The Sustainable Development Goals Report.* UN, 2020. Retrieved from: https://unstats.un.org/sdgs/report/2020/

103 *The Second Growth and Transformation Plan (GTP II) Midterm Review Report.* Addis Ababa: National Planning Commission, June 2018.

104 *Third Five-Year Development Plan of Ethiopia (1968–1973).* Addis Ababa: Berhannena Selam Printing Press,1968.

105 Todaro, Michael. *Economic Development in the Third World.* New York: Longman Inc, 1986.

106 Trading Economics 2020. Retrieved from: https://tradingeconomics.com/country- list/inflation-rate

107 Trines, Stefan. "Education in Ethiopia," *World Education News + Reviews* (WENR), November 15, 2018. Retrieved from: https://wenr.wes.org/2018/11/education-in-ethiopia

108 UNESCO (2019). Retrieved from: https://tellmaps.com/uis/oosc/#!/tellmap/406451723/0

109 UNESCO, World Heritage Center. Retrieved from: https://whc.unesco.org/en/statesparties/et

110 UNICEF, April 9, 2020. Retrieved from: https://www.unicef. org/ethiopia/press-releases/more-half-children-remain-exclud ed-pre-primary-education-ethiopia-despite-impressive

111 UNICEF, 2019. Retrieved from: https://tellmaps.com/uis/gender/#!/ tellmap/51170220/3

112 UN/DESA Policy Brief #53: Reflection on development policy in the 1970s and 1980s. August 25, 2017. Retrieved from: https://www.un.org/development/desa/dpad/publication/ policy-brief-53-reflection-on-   development-policy-in-the-1970 s-and-1980s/

113 UNIDO, Sept. 17, 2020. Retrieved from: https://www.unido.org/ stories/what-industrialization-means-well-being--and- why-it- matters

114 United Nations. Retrieved from https://www.un.org/en/sections/ issues-depth/poverty/

115 U.N. Environment Programme. "Air pollution hurts the poorest most." May 9, 2019. Retrieved from: https://www.unenvironment. org/news-and-stories/story/air-pollution-hurts-poorest-most

116 U.N. Environment, Dec. 2017. Retrieved from: https://www. unenvironment.org/news-and-stories/press-release/resource-us e-expected-double-2050-better-natural-resource-use

117 U.N. Rural Organizations, Ethiopia, April 1973.

118 U.N. World Food Program (2020). Retrieved from: https://www.wfp. org/countries/ethiopia

119 UNDP, Global Multidimensional Poverty Index. Retrieved from: http://hdr.undp.org/sites/default/files/mpi 2019 publication.pdf

120 USAID News, May 8, 2020. Retrieved from: https://www.usaid.gov/ news- information

121 U.S. Bureau of Labor Statistics. Retrieved from: https://www.bls. gov/cpi/

122 *Why Corruption Matters: understanding causes, effectiveness and how to address them.* The UK Department for International Development, January 2015. Retrieved from: https://www.gov.uk/government/ organisations/department-for-international- development

123 WITS Trade Data, 2016. Retrieved from: https://wits.worldbank.org/CountryProfile/en/Country/ETH/Year/LTST/Summary

124 World Bank. *Migration and Remittances Fact Book, 2016* (3rd ed.). Retrieved from: https://openknowledge.worldbank.org/handle/10986/23743

125 World Bank. *Doing Business 2020.* Retrieved from: https://www.doingbusiness.org/en/doingbusiness

126 World Bank. *Special Topic: Poverty & Household Welfare in Ethiopia, 2011–2016.* Retrieved from: http://documents1.worldbank.org/curated/en/432421554200542956/pdf/Special-Topic-Poverty-and-Household-Welfare-in-Ethiopia-2011-2016.pdf

127 World Development Report, 1990.

128 World Economic Forum, Feb. 3, 2020. Retrieved from: https://www.weforum.org/agenda/2020/02/global-corruption-transparency-international-index/

129 World Bank News, June 17, 2020. Retrieved from https://www.worldbank.org/ World Bank, sept 19, 2018. Retrieved from: https://www.worldbank.org/en/news/press-release/2018/09/19/decline-of-global-extreme-poverty-continues-but-has-slowed-world-bank

130 World Bank (Modeled ILO Estimate), 2020. Retrieved from: https://data.worldbank.org/indicator/SL.UEM.TOTL.ZS

131 World Economic Forum, Dec.7, 2016. Retrieved from: https://www.weforum.org/agenda/2016/12/this-map-shows-how-much-each-country-spends-on-food/

132 World Economic Forum, Jan. 23, 2015. Retrieved from: https://www.weforum.org/agenda/2015/01/want-to-end-poverty-start-with-corruption/

133 Worldometer, 2019. Retrieved from: https://www.worldometers.info/world-population/ethiopia-population/

APPENDIX

APPENDIX

APPENDIX 1 HUMAN DEVELOPMENT INDEX

Ethiopia

Life expectancy at birth (years)	66.2
Adult mortality rate, female (per 1,000 people)	189
Adult mortality rate, male (per 1,000 people)	240
Age-standardized mortality rates attributed to noncommunicable diseases, female	522.9
Age-standardized mortality rates attributed to noncommunicable diseases, male	589.8
Child malnutrition, stunting (moderate or severe) (% under age 5)	38.4
Current health expenditure (% of GDP)	4
Life expectancy at birth, female (years)	68.2
Life expectancy at birth, male (years)	64.3
Life expectancy index	0.711
HIV prevalence, adult (% ages 15-49)	0.9
Mortality rate, infant (per 1,000 live births)	41
Infants lacking immunization, DPT (% of one-year-olds)	15
Infants lacking immunization, measles (% of one-year-olds)	39
Malaria incidence (per 1,000 people at risk)	37.4
Tuberculosis incidence (per 100,000 people)	164
Mortality rate, under-five (per 1,000 live births)	58.5
Expected years of schooling (years)	8.7
Education index	0.335
Expected years of schooling, female (years)	8.3
Expected years of schooling, male (years)	9.1

Government expenditure on education (% of GDP)	4.7
Gross enrollment ratio, pre-primary (% of preschool-age children)	30
Gross enrollment ratio, primary (% of primary school-age population)	102
Gross enrollment ratio, secondary (% of secondary school-age population)	35
Gross enrollment ratio, tertiary (% of tertiary school-age population)	8
Literacy rate, adult (% ages 15 and older)	n.a.
Mean years of schooling (years)	2.8
Mean years of schooling, female (years)	1.6
Mean years of schooling, male (years)	3.9
Percentage of primary schools with access to the internet	n.a.
Percentage of secondary schools with access to the internet	n.a.
Population with at least some secondary education (% ages 25 and older)	17.1
Population with at least some secondary education, female (% ages 25 and older)	11.5
Population with at least some secondary education, male (% ages 25 and older)	22
Primary school dropout rate (% of primary school cohort)	61.8
Primary school teachers trained to teach (%)	85
Program for International Student Assessment (PISA) score in mathematics	n.a.
Program for International Student Assessment (PISA) score in reading	n.a.

Program for International Student Assessment (PISA) score in science	n.a.
Pupil-teacher ratio, primary school (number of pupils per teacher)	n.a.
Survival rate to the last grade of lower secondary general education (%)	68
Gross national income (GNI) per capita (2011 PPP $)	1,782
Domestic credit provided by financial sector (% of GDP)	n.a.
Gross domestic product (GDP) per capita (2011 PPP $)	1,794
Gross domestic product (GDP), total (2011 PPP $ billions)	196
Gross fixed capital formation (% of GDP)	34.1
Income index	0.435
Labor share of GDP, comprising wages and social protection transfers (%)	n.a.
Inequality-adjusted HDI (IHDI)	0.337
Coefficient of human inequality	27.2
Income inequality, Gini coefficient	39.1
Income inequality, Palma ratio	1.8
Income inequality, quintile ratio	7.1
Income share held by poorest 40%	17.6
Income share held by richest 1%	n.a.
Income share held by richest 10%	31.4
Inequality in education (%)	43.5
Inequality in income (%)	13.4
Inequality in life expectancy (%)	24.9
Inequality-adjusted education index	0.189
Inequality-adjusted income index	0.377
Inequality-adjusted life expectancy index	0.534

Overall loss in HDI due to inequality (%) 28.4

Gender Development Index (GDI) 0.844

Adolescent birth rate (births per 66.7
1,000 women ages 15-19)

Antenatal care coverage, at least one visit (%) 62.4

Child marriage, women married by age 18 (% of women
ages 20–24 years who are married or in union)

Contraceptive prevalence, any method 40.1
(% of married or in-union women of
reproductive age, 15–49 years)

Estimated gross national income per 1,332
capita, female (2011 PPP $)

Estimated gross national income 2,231
per capita, male (2011 PPP $)

Female share of employment in senior 21.1
and middle management (%)

Female share of graduates in science, 7.6
technology, engineering and mathematics
programs at tertiary level (%)

Gender Inequality Index (GII) 0.508

Human Development Index (HDI), female 0.428

Human Development Index (HDI), male 0.507

Mandatory paid maternity leave (days) 90

Maternal mortality ratio (deaths 353
per 100,000 live births)

Prevalence of female genital mutilation/ 65.2
cutting among girls and women (% of
girls and young women ages 15-49)

Proportion of births attended by 27.7
skilled health personnel (%)

Share of employment in nonagriculture, female (% of total employment in nonagriculture)	55.6
Share of graduates from science, technology, engineering and mathematics programs in tertiary education who are female (%)	17.3
Share of graduates from STEM programs in tertiary education who are male (%)	82.7
Share of seats in parliament (% held by women)	37.3
Total unemployment rate (female to male ratio)	1.85
Unmet need for family planning (% of married or in-union women of reproductive age, 15-49 years)	20.6
Violence against women ever experienced, intimate partner (% of female population ages 15 and older)	28
Violence against women ever experienced, nonintimate partner (% of female population ages 15 and older)	n.a.
Women with account at financial institution or with mobile money-service provider (% of female population ages 15 and older)	29.1
Youth unemployment rate (female to male ratio)	1.8
Population in multidimensional poverty, headcount (%)	83.5
Contribution of deprivation in education to the Multidimensional Poverty Index	29.4
Contribution of deprivation in health to the Multidimensional Poverty Index	19.7
Contribution of deprivation in standard of living to the Multidimensional Poverty Index	50.8
Multidimensional Poverty Index (MPI)	0.489
Population in multidimensional poverty, headcount (thousands) (for the year of survey)	85,510.60

Population in multidimensional poverty, headcount (thousands) (projection for 2017)	87,643.50
Population in multidimensional poverty, intensity of deprivation (%)	58.5
Population in severe multidimensional poverty (%)	61.5
Population living below income poverty line, PPP $1.90 a day (%)	27.3
Population living below income poverty line, national poverty line (%)	23.5
Population vulnerable to multidimensional poverty (%)	8.9
Working poor at PPP$3.10 a day (% of total employment)	56.1
Employment to population ratio (% ages 15 and older)	78.9
Child labor (% ages 5-17)	48.6
Employment in agriculture (% of total employment)	66.2
Employment in services (% of total employment)	21.8
Labor force participation rate (% ages 15 and older)	80.3
Labor force participation rate (% ages 15 and older), female	74.2
Labor force participation rate (% ages 15 and older), male	86.5
Old-age pension recipients (% of statutory pension age population)	15.3
Unemployment, total (% of labor force)	1.8
Proportion of informal employment in nonagricultural employment (% of total employment in nonagriculture)	n.a.
Unemployment, youth (% ages 15-24)	2.8
Vulnerable employment (% of total employment)	86

Youth not in school or employment (% ages 15-24)   10.5
Homicide rate (per 100,000 people)   n.a.
Birth registration (% under age 5)   3
Homeless people due to natural disaster   2
(average annual per million people)
Prison population (per 100,000 people)   117
Refugees by country of origin (thousands)   92.2
Suicide rate, female (per 100,000 people)   4.7
Suicide rate, male (per 100,000 people)   18.7
Exports and imports (% of GDP)   31.2
Foreign direct investment, net inflows (% of GDP)   4.9
Net official development assistance   5.1
received (% of GNI)
Private capital flows (% of GDP)   n.a.
Remittances, inflows (% of GDP)   0.49
Internet users, total (% of population)   18.6
International inbound tourists (thousands)   933
International student mobility (%   n.a.
of total tertiary enrollment)
Internet users, female (% of female population)   n.a.
Mobile phone subscriptions (per 100 people)   37.2
Net migration rate (per 1,000 people)   0.3
Carbon dioxide emissions, per capita (tonnes)   0.1
Carbon dioxide emissions (kg per 2010 US$ of GDP)   0.07
Forest area (% of total land area)   12.5
Degraded land (% of total land area)   29
Forest area, change (%)   n.a.
Fossil fuel energy consumption (%   6.6
of total energy consumption)
Fresh water withdrawals (% of total   8.7
renewable water resources)

Mortality rate attributed to household and ambient air pollution (per 100,000 population) — 144

Mortality rate attributed to unsafe water, sanitation and hygiene services (per 100,000 population) — 43.7

Natural resource depletion (% of GNI) — 9.4

Red List Index (value) — 0.842

Renewable energy consumption (% of total final energy consumption) — 92.2

Total population (millions) — 109.2

Median age (years) — 19.5

Old-age (65 and older) dependency ratio (per 100 people ages 15-64) — 6.3

Population ages 15-64 (millions) — 60.9

Population ages 65 and older (millions) — 3.8

Population under age 5 (millions) — 16.3

Sex ratio at birth (male to female births) — 1.04

Urban population (%) — 20.8

Young age (0-14) dependency ratio (per 100 people ages 15-64) — 73.2

Skilled labor force (% of labor force) — 6.8

Adjusted net savings (% of GNI) — 9.3

Average annual change in the share of bottom 40% (%) — -2.2

Concentration index (exports) (value) — 0.298

Gross capital formation (% of GDP) — 34.1

Overall loss in HDI value due to inequality, average annual change (%) — -2.2

Population using improved drinking-water sources (%) — 41

Population using improved sanitation facilities (%) — 7

Ratio of education and health expenditure   12.4
to military expenditure

Research and development expenditure (% of GDP)   0.6

Rural population with access to electricity (%)   31

Total debt service (% of exports of goods,   20.8
services and primary income)

Source: UN, Human Development Report 2019 http://hdr.undp.org/en/
countries/profiles/ETH#

APPENDIX 2 GINI - COEFFICIENT & RELATED INDICATORS

	Last	Previous	Frequency
ET: Gini Coefficient (GINI Index): World Bank Estimate (%)	39.10	33.20	Yearly
	2015	2010	
ET: Income Share Held by Fourth 20% (%)	20.60	21.30	Yearly
	2015	2010	
ET: Income Share Held by Highest 10% (%)	31.40	27.40	Yearly
	2015	2010	
ET: Income Share Held by Highest 20% (%)	46.70	41.70	Yearly
	2015	2010	
ET: Income Share Held by Lowest 10% (%)	2.60	3.20	Yearly
	2015	2010	
ET: Income Share Held by Lowest 20% (%)	6.60	8.00	Yearly
	2015	2010	
ET: Income Share Held by Second 20% (%)	11.00	12.60	Yearly
	2015	2010	
ET: Income Share Held by Third 20% (%)	15.00	16.30	Yearly
	2015	2010	
ET: Poverty Gap at $1.90 a Day: 2011 PPP: % (%)	7.70	9.10	Yearly
	2015	2010	

ET: Poverty Gap at $3.20 a Day: 2011 PPP: % (%)	22.70	28.00	Yearly
	2015	2010	
ET: Poverty Gap at $5.50 a Day: 2011 PPP: % (%)	45.00	52.20	Yearly
	2015	2010	
ET: Poverty Gap at National Poverty Lines: % (%)	7.80	8.30	Yearly
	2010	2004	
ET: Poverty Gap at National Poverty Lines: Rural: % (%)	8.00	8.50	Yearly
	2010	2004	
ET: Poverty Gap at National Poverty Lines: Urban: % (%)	6.90	7.70	Yearly
	2010	2004	
ET: Poverty Headcount Ratio at $1.90 a Day: 2011 PPP: % of Population (%)	26.70	33.60	Yearly
	2015	2010	
ET: Poverty Headcount Ratio at $3.20 a Day: 2011 PPP: % of Population (%)	61.40	73.10	Yearly
	2015	2010	
ET: Poverty Headcount Ratio at $5.50 a Day: 2011 PPP: % of Population (%)	84.70	93.10	Yearly
	2015	2010	
ET: Poverty Headcount Ratio at National Poverty Lines: % of Population (%)	29.60	38.90	Yearly
	2010	2004	

ET: Poverty Headcount Ratio at National Poverty Lines: Rural: % of Rural Pop. (%)	30.40	39.30	Yearly
	2010	2004	
ET: Poverty Headcount Ratio at National Poverty Lines: Urban: % of Urban Pop. (%)	25.70	35.10	Yearly
	2010	2004	

Source:
https://www.ceicdata.com/en/ethiopia/poverty/et-gini-coefficient-gini-index-world-bank-estimate
retrieved on July 20,2020

APPENDIX 3 FISCAL AND MONETARY POLICY OF ETHIOPIA (PRIOR TO 1980)

The Ethiopian fiscal and monetary policies have hindered employment expansion. Regarding monetary policy, a fixed exchange rate was retained to maintain the country's international reserves. As a result, aggregate demand had to be balanced to the level compatible with foreign exchange earnings resulting from coffee export. And when coffee prices declined, the monetary authorities resorted to a tightened money supply to reduce aggregate demand. In essence, tight monetary policy led to "industrial sales declines, increases in inventories, and underutilization of installed capacity"[181]

To avoid this situation, aggregate demand could be stimulated by applying easy monetary policy. It means that the Ethiopian Birr must be devalued to support the substitution of imported goods with labor-intensive manufactured goods produced in the country. In addition, the export of agricultural products could be encouraged provided that domestic currency was supported by devaluation. With respect to fiscal policy, the import substitution strategy embraced high tariff structure to protect infant industries. The Ethiopian tariff on imported good exceeded 50%, while a 30% tariff was expected to be reasonable for less developed countries.[182]

"Rigid adherence to an import substitution policy makes it impossible to develop exports different from the

---

[181] ILO, *Employment and Unemployment in Ethiopia* (Geneva, 1974), 23.

[182] Ibid.

traditional primary products in which these countries have clear comparative advantage."[183] The tariff structure was also a barrier to employment creation in Ethiopia, "because most capital goods, capable of displacing labor, carried a zero duty, while the simple tools which are a complement to labor, carried positive duties."[184]

Therefore, to encourage employment expansion in Ethiopia, the tax on imported goods had to be lowered and tariff should have been imposed on capital goods, relative to simple tools.

---

[183] Ibid.

[184] Ibid.

APPENDIX 4 LABOR FORCE TREND IN ETHIOPIA

Year	Labor Force	
	(in million)	(% Δ)
2010	39	----
2011	40.6	4.1
2012	42	3.4
2013	43.6	3.8
2014	45	3.2
2015	46.7	3.8
2016	48	2.8
2017	49.8	3.8
2018	51.4	3.2
2019	53	3.1
2020	52.8	-3.8

Source: World Bank, based on I
LO ILOSTAT database.
Retrieved on Jan 29, 2021
(% Δ-author's computation)

Projection for ten years (2020-2030)
∑% Δ = (4.1+3.4+3.8+3.2+3.8+2.8+3.8+3.2+3.1-3.8) =27.4
Average labor force growth rate (2010-2020) =27.4/10 =2.74%

187

Using this into the following formula:

LF2030 = LFA 2020 $(1+\Delta L)^n$

Where: LF = Labor force

LFA (2010-2020) = 46.5 million(average)

ΔL= Labor force growth rate

n= the number of years, (2020-2030) =10

Inserting the above values into the formula,

we have:

LF2030 = 52.8 $(1.027)^{10}$

LFA 2010-2020 = 46.5 million (1.31) = <u>61 million</u>

Considering labor growth to be compatible with population growth (2.6%),

LF2030 = 46.5 $(1.026)^{10}$ = 46.5 (1.29) = <u>60 million</u>

APPENDIX 5 POVERTY REDUCTION LESSONS

Appendix 5 provides a snapshot of the experiences of countries that have reduced poverty. Brazil, Norway, and China are selected.

1. Brazil

Brazil, famous for its football, embarked on poverty reduction programs and reduced poverty by initiating a series of measures. According to the World Bank, Brazil slashed poverty in half.[185] The Borgen Report[186] identifies Brazil's poverty alleviation programs as follows:

World Without Poverty was initiated in 2013 to reduce poverty by creating social programs. It evolved into *"Bolsa Familia,"* providing immediate poverty assistance for families, and encouraging families to send their children to school and comply with required health checkups. Brazil Without Misery was introduced in 2011 to help families earning less than $70 a month and lifted 22 million people out of poverty.

a. "Rural Poverty Reduction Program" was designed to empower people in rural communities and help them to participate in local decisions,

b. "Zero Hunger Program" was rolled out to provide financial support to farmers and to feed school children.

---

[185] "How to Reduce Poverty: A New Lesson from Brazil for the world?" World Bank, March 22, 2014.

[186] "Five stages for Poverty reduction in Brazil," *Borgen Magazine,* Feb. 23, 2018.

The program reduced children-malnutrition from 12.7 percent to 3.5 percent, and

c. "National Program for Access to Technical Education and Employment" was introduced to provide free public education so that Brazilian children can enhance their technical knowledge.

2. Norway

A Scandinavian country, Norway has achieved remarkable progress on the economic and social fronts. In 2017, it ranked number one as the most inclusive economy. "It has the lowest income inequality in the world, helped by a mix of policies that support education and innovation"[187]

Index of Inclusive Economies – 2017

Country	Ranking
Norway	1
Luxembourg	2
Switzerland	3
Iceland	4
Denmark	5
Sweden	6
Netherlands	7
Australia	8
New Zealand	9
Austria	10

Source: World Economic Forum

---

[187] World Economic Forum, April 12, 2017.

The lesson we can draw from Norway is that introducing and implementing inclusive quality education is crucial for sustained economic development. Norway[188] is also among the ten least corrupt countries in the world, with a Corruption Perception Index (CPI) of 84/100; the focus is on promoting inclusive economic growth. Acemoglu and Robinson highlight the importance of inclusive economic and political institutions, which allow individuals to make better choices in decision making: inclusive institutions "have the capacity and incentive to enforce rules and regulations, and political power that are much more broadly spread."[189]

3. China

China has gone through years of deliberate efforts aimed at alleviating poverty. Now it is approaching its goal. "The number of poor people is estimated to have fallen from about 200 million in 1981 to 28 million in 2002."[190] And according to the National Bureau of Statistics (NBS) of China, "the number of impoverished people dropped from 770 million to 16.6 million, and the poverty rate dropped from 97.5 percent to 1.7 percent from 1978 to 2018, making significant contribution to the UN's

[188] Transparency International data.

[189] Daron Acemoglu and James A. Robinson, *Rents and economic development: the perspective of Why Nations Fail*, (Public Choice, 2019), 20.

[190] Wang Sangui, Li Zhou, and Ren Yanshun, *8-7 National Poverty Reduction Program in China – The National Strategy and Its Impact*, World Bank, 3.

Millennium Development Goals and providing inspirations for global poverty alleviation governance."[191]

China introduced a series of poverty alleviation programs. First, it rolled out a rural reform program (1978–1985), which contributed to growth in grain yield and higher rural income. Second, the National Targeted Poverty Reduction programs (1986–1993) took place. However, 80 million rural population remained poor. The Chinese government initiated the 8-7 Plan (National Plan for Poverty Reduction) to lift 80 million poor Chinese out of poverty during the period 1994–2000. According to the plan, "poor household[s] were assisted with land improvement, increased cash crop, tree crop and livestock production"[192] Then poverty reduction Strategy in the New Century (2001–2010) was introduced with the aim of targeting poverty at county and village levels. International Organizations and local NGOs also contributed to poverty reduction in China. International Organizations and local NGOs also contributed to poverty reduction in China.

International organizations contributing
to poverty reduction in China

International	
Development	UNDP, FAO, WFP, UNICEF, UNIDO, ILO, UNFPA
Agencies	
International	

---

[191] *China's success in poverty alleviation: Lessons for other Countries*, World Bank, Sept. 20, 2019.

[192] Sangui et al., *8-7 National Poverty Reduction Program*, 10.

Financial Institutions	IBRD, ADB, IFAD
Bilateral Agencies/ Governments	AusAID, CIDA, DFID, GTZ, JICA, The Netherlands, Finland, Sweden
International NGOs	The Ford Foundation, WWW, Oxfam Hong Kong, KFW, Aide Foundation, World Vision, Save the Children of Britain, International Programs, the International Crane Foundation, Trick-up USA

Source: Sangui et al., *8-7 National Poverty Reduction Program*, 34.

The Chinese government has also relocated poor families within China and provided shelter and basic needs. In addition to international agencies, local NGOs have also participated in poverty reduction activities in China.

Chinese NGOs and Their Poverty Reduction Activities

NGOs	Poverty reduction Activities
China Foundation for Poverty Alleviation	Micro-credit, capacity building, applicable technology extension, emergence relief, healthcare for women and children, and primary education
China Charity Federation	Income generation activities, relief medical subsidies, subsidies for students & schools, professional technical training

Women's poverty reduction action of the All China Women's Federation	Technical training, micro-credit, paired assistance, labor migration, assistance for female students, small scale infrastructure construction and healthcare for women
China's Disabled Persons Federation	Applicable technical training, micro-credit, repair of endangered house, establishment of service center
Project Hope of the China Youth Development Foundation	Fellowship for dropout children from school, construction of hope primary school, teachers' training, teaching equipment
China Society for Promotion of the Glorious Cause	Project investment, donation for education, and support for other public affairs
Happiness project of the China Popular Welfare Foundation, the China Family Planning, Association of the China Population News Press	Micro-credit
Song Quingling Foundation	subsidies for female students, construction of primary and middle schools, library on wheels for children, fellowship for female students attending normal colleges, teachers' training, and reward fund for teachers
Microfinance center of the Chinese Academy of Social Sciences	Micro-credit and micro-credit training

Source: Sangui et al., 8-7 National Poverty Reduction Program, 33

ABOUT THE AUTHOR

Dr. Assefa Muluneh served as a senior economist at the Planning Office in Addis Ababa, Ethiopia. He has pursued his career in development economics and participated in job creation programs, in collaboration with International Labor Organization's team of experts. He is engaged as a professor of economics and in research and scholarly activities in the United States.